THE *Arts*

Inspected

Contents

Foreword

Jim Rose HMI

DIRECTOR OF INSPECTION

INSPECTION is largely an eye-witness event. It builds judgements from close observations of how pupils respond to what teachers do to foster learning and promote high standards of work.

The Arts Inspected describes and comments upon work where good teaching results in high standards in art, dance, drama and music. It shows how teachers who are specialists in these subjects, and those who are not, plan, prepare and teach worthwhile programmes of work in the arts for pupils in primary and secondary schools. The work amply illustrates the benefits of a rich arts curriculum for all pupils.

We wish to thank all those schools whose work we have drawn upon for this publication and hope it will be of interest to teachers and to those who provide for these subjects in schools.

OFSTED has produced an appendix to this book that includes examples of pupils' work in some of the schools listed and is available through the Internet. It can be accessed through OFSTED's home page: http://www.ofsted.gov.uk

1 Introduction

'*Art is the expression of the profoundest thoughts in the simplest way.*'
ALBERT EINSTEIN

Good arts teaching

The Office for Standards in Education (OFSTED) is a government department that seeks to promote *improvement through inspection*. One of its approaches to improvement is the dissemination of good practice revealed by school inspection. The aspect of practice that forms the focus of this book is good teaching in arts subjects. It has been written mainly for an audience of primary and secondary teachers who teach one or more arts subjects, but may also be of interest to others with a commitment to the arts or education, for example school governors, parents, school inspectors and professional artists.

This book is concerned with good practice, rather than best practice. Some of the points made are illustrated with brief references to aspects of the arts work in specific schools. The book does not aim to tell the full story of the good arts practice in any of these schools. Neither does it aim to present these schools as better than all the other schools in England. The schools that are named include some that arguably could be numbered among the best schools for the arts in the country. Others with similar qualities may have been omitted.

During the academic years 1995–96 and 1996–97 over 10,000 primary, secondary and special schools were inspected by registered inspectors, additional inspectors or HM Inspectors under Section 10 of the School Inspections Act 1996[1]. All these inspections addressed arts subjects. The findings from Section 10 inspections were used as a backdrop for some focused inspection of art, dance, drama or music in 98 schools where there was a strong likelihood of good practice. Most of these inspections lasted one day and were carried out by HM Inspectors; some visits were made by additional inspectors. For simplicity, the accounts of good practice observed during these inspections have been divided into four freestanding chapters (Chapters

2–5) that nominally address art, dance, drama and music separately, and are structured to fit the subject in question. However, because of the strong links between the arts, readers will find that each chapter includes examples that draw on more than one arts subject. Some of the issues that arise from the subject chapters are drawn together in Chapter 6, which concludes the book.

This publication forms part of OFSTED's response to the 'Arts and Young People Initiative' of the Department of National Heritage[2]. OFSTED's full commitment was published in *Setting the Scene* (DNH 1996). The focus on art, dance, drama and music in the present volume was intended to mirror *Setting the Scene*. Future work on the arts in OFSTED will also address other aspects of the arts, such as poetry.

What is good teaching?

The *Framework for the Inspection of Schools* (OFSTED 1995a) defines the quality of teaching in terms of its effect on pupils' attainment. Good teaching enables pupils to make good progress. The criteria that inspectors address when evaluating the quality of teaching in a school include the extent to which teachers:

1 have a secure knowledge and understanding of the subjects they teach;

2 set high expectations so as to challenge pupils and deepen their knowledge and understanding;

3 plan effectively;

4 employ methods and organisational strategies which match curricular objectives and the needs of all pupils;

5 manage pupils well and achieve high standards of discipline;

6 use time and resources effectively;

7 assess pupils' work thoroughly and constructively, and use assessments to inform teaching;

8 use homework effectively to reinforce and/or extend what is learned in school.
(OFSTED 1995a)

Inspectors apply these criteria consistently when making judgements about the quality of teaching in individual lessons. Clearly, the first six criteria apply to almost any lesson. On the other hand, it would not be sensible to expect every lesson in a school to include formal assessment of all pupils' work (criterion 7), or the setting of formal homework tasks (criterion 8). However, aspects of these criteria may still apply. If high expectations (criterion 2) have arisen through effective planning (criterion 3), rather than by chance, it follows that some sort of assessment is being used to inform the teaching (criterion 7). If the pupils have been enthused, as well as challenged (criterion 2), they may use time outside lessons to reinforce and extend their learning on their own initiative, or in response to an informal suggestion from a teacher (criterion 8).

The criteria define the broad qualities that examples of good teaching have in common. At a more detailed level, the characteristics of the good teaching that is present in different schools, or at different times in the same school, may vary widely. Some good lessons maintain a fast pace throughout, while others alter the pace of the work, sometimes requiring an immediate response and at other times allowing more time for reflection. In some good lessons there is a wide range of resources available; in others all pupils may use identical equipment, or none at all. High standards of discipline are achieved in many ways. Different teachers may not use exactly the same methods and organisational strategies to achieve similar curricular objectives.

The examples of arts teaching that are described in this book meet the criteria that are listed in the *Framework for Inspection*. Thereafter, they tell some quite different stories. It is hoped that readers who are teachers will find these insights into other teachers' approaches helpful as they seek to develop and improve the arts teaching in their own school.

Why teach the arts?

No book on arts education would be complete without at least a brief justification of the place of the arts in education.

Schools might be said to teach the arts because they have to. The National Curriculum requires that all maintained schools teach dance (as part of physical education) in Key Stages 1 and 2, art and music in Key Stages 1 to 3, and drama (as part of English) in Key Stages 1 to 4. However, many schools substantially exceed these requirements in several respects. It would have been difficult, moreover, to find a school that did not teach most, if not all, of these subjects prior to the introduction of the National Curriculum. Obviously, the reasons for teaching the arts are not only to comply with the law.

Some might justify the place of the arts in the curriculum on the grounds that involvement in the arts can lead to higher attainment in other subjects. This is a rationale that deserves serious consideration. Recent research studies have suggested that there can be a link between education in the arts and pupils' attainment in English or mathematics. For example, in the United States, Gardiner, Fox, Knowles and Jeffrey (1996) found that 96 pupils aged 5–7 years who participated in a music and art curriculum 'which emphasised sequenced skill development' progressed more rapidly in mathematics and reading than a control group who followed their normal art and music curriculum. The researchers argued that the result arose because:

- the motivating effects of learning arts skills led the pupils to improve their attitudes to learning and school
- the mental *stretching* required by the arts transferred to other areas of learning.

However, the most persuasive argument for an education in the arts concerns the benefits of attainment in the arts for its own sake.

- The arts, defined in this context as art, dance, drama and music, are intrinsic components of human culture, heritage and creativity. They mirror the whole repertoire of human experience, and are worthy of study in their own right. It is difficult to imagine a world without arts, with no drawing, music or painting for example. Few, if any, cultures are without these elements.

- The arts are a response to our thirst for knowledge, insight and revelation. They give people opportunities to explore their feelings, come into contact with the spiritual, increase their knowledge, develop their skills, and articulate and realise their aspirations. They provide ways of knowing, representing, presenting, interpreting and symbolising, and a context for appreciating and valuing.

- Contact with the arts requires the abilities to question, explore, collaborate, and extend and develop one's ideas, and the ideas of others. The creation of art requires a sense of structure, discipline, rigour, and a positive response to challenge.

Notes

[1] Previously Section 9 of the Education (Schools) Act 1992.

[2] Now the Department for Culture, Media and Sport (DCMS).

2 Art

Peter Jones HMI

SPECIALIST ADVISER FOR ART

ART is a compulsory subject within the National Curriculum in England (DFE 1995) for all pupils in Key Stages 1 to 3, and is interpreted as art, craft and design throughout. Pupils' understanding and enjoyment of art are developed through activities that bring together, where possible, requirements from the two Attainment Targets: AT1 Investigating and Making, and AT2 Knowledge and Understanding. Pupils should be given opportunities to experience different approaches to art, including those that involve working individually, in groups and as a whole class. The programmes of study for the three key stages indicate how pupils should learn the practical skills of art progressively through working in two and three dimensions with pattern and texture, colour, line and tone, shape, form and space. They also show how they should be introduced to a selection of the work of artists, craftspeople and designers. There is considerable scope for teachers and pupils to make choices about the styles and genres they study within the categories of work from the locality, the past and present, and a variety of Western and non-Western cultures.

At Key Stage 4 more than one-third of Year 10 and 11 pupils take art or art and design as a GCSE subject. The syllabuses allow pupils to develop practical and critical skills, in most cases through a range of two- and three-dimensional work.

Sixth-form work is traditionally examined through A-level art, with its focus on the development of pupils' capacity for more personal expression, and the in-depth study of the work of artists. However, increasing numbers of students are taking a GNVQ (General National Vocational Qualification) in art and design, with an emphasis on the application of art in a business context.

The examples of work in this chapter meet and sometimes go beyond the requirements of the National Curriculum and public examinations, but they cannot cover in detail all the most important recent developments in art in schools. For example, excellent work in the use of computer graphics, video and digital cameras and colour printers is now both enhancing existing art skills and subtly shifting teachers' views on how pupils learn in and through art. These developments are touched on here, and are described more fully in a forthcoming publication on art and IT (NCET in press). Some schools now see how important art is in giving pupils the opportunity to explore issues and express beliefs and personal convictions. Crucial to this development is the way in which teachers can set work which demands more than just technical skills, and which calls on pupils to think about the meaning of art and the values it expresses.

The schools described in this chapter vary in their stages of development in art. They show in their different ways how improvements can be made to teaching art, and how art can strengthen work in other subjects. All the schools have a sound rationale for art in the curriculum, and central to this is the vision and commitment of the teachers – they believe that art really matters in children's education, that it can make a difference to the way children see, understand and appreciate the world. The teachers are inventive and resourceful in achieving success: they plan skilfully, they organise materials and equipment meticulously, they make their classrooms into attractive environments with displays of pupils' work and of artefacts, they capitalise on children's curiosity and their readiness to experiment, and they do not shrink from teaching the knowledge and skills necessary for children to make good progress and attain high standards.

Art in primary schools

OFSTED's evidence (Jones 1997) shows that where standards of attainment in primary art are good, pupils:

- learn to use a wide range of materials in two and three dimensions and develop skills in handling them safely
- experiment in colour, line and texture
- begin to draw from observation at an early stage
- make significant progress in the development of a range of skills, particularly in drawing
- show increasing awareness of compositional and design possibilities
- have an understanding of artistic processes and techniques, and are encouraged to look at the work of artists as sources of inspiration and aids to developing their own skills and techniques
- use sketchbooks for making visual notes which are used later as starting points for other work
- discuss their work confidently and enjoy using technical terms to describe it.

Art is essentially a practical subject that requires a good deal of attention to preparation as well as planning. It is not uncommon to find well-planned lessons which are unsuccessful because of poor preparation of the practical materials required for the work and poor access to them. The good work described below invariably stems from sound planning *and* thorough preparation of the resources required for the work to progress from simple to more complex ideas.

The basic resources for art, including mark-making materials and media for two- and three-dimensional work, usefully service a number of other subjects. The disciplined and organised use of these materials was a notable feature of the good work, none of which was 'accidental'. The teachers, and teaching assistants where available, worked effectively to plan and prepare lessons and agreed, for example, how to teach pupils to be creative but economical with expendable materials.

It is all too obvious that good planning and thorough preparation free the teacher to teach. Where these basic features are weak, otherwise effective teachers are hampered by having to attend to problems, such as the distribution of materials and tools for art during the lesson, which could have been solved by better preparation.

It is also obvious in the good lessons that the pupils learn to take responsibility for organizing themselves and their workspace with commendable self-discipline.

Most secondary art teachers have graduate qualifications in the subject, and are able to concentrate almost solely on the teaching of art. However, for the vast majority of primary teachers art is just one of the subjects within the National Curriculum which they must teach.

The examples of primary art given here do not assume that primary teachers are specialists in the subject. What they show is the merit of careful thought about teaching and learning art, and the value of clear expectations and judgements about outcomes. For example, in teaching drawing, much can be achieved when the teacher understands the stages children go through in learning to draw, and manages the work

accordingly. The pupils develop confidence in their drawing skills through regularly working from observation, from memory and from imagination. The teacher provides good visual stimuli and makes sure that the pupils understand the task. The materials and equipment provided are well suited to the task and offer pupils an element of choice. The teacher looks carefully and critically at work in progress, intervening to make teaching points, to challenge pupils and to raise their standards, using knowledge and experience to predict the direction the pupils' work will take. Work is discussed with the whole class, with small groups and with individuals, and at the end of the session pupils are encouraged to talk about what has been achieved.

The characteristics of good teaching in primary schools observed during inspection include that:

- a sequence of lessons is thoroughly planned
- classroom assistants share the planning of lessons and understand the learning objectives
- resources are well organised, and materials and equipment are accessible when needed
- lessons are targeted on teaching specific skills
- the purpose of the lesson is fully explained to the pupils
- the introduction is supported by well-chosen visual resources
- the teacher demonstrates a practical technique confidently
- pupils receive focused support from the teacher and classroom assistants

- individual, group and class discussion of the work helps in its assessment
- the teacher evaluates and monitors both the process and outcomes of the lesson so that planning for progression can be systematic
- the quality of display does justice to the high standards of pupils' work, and provides both a learning resource and an assessment tool.

The examples show how, even in schools which face considerable difficulties in the quality of their environment or resources, well-taught art can transform a requirement into a source of pleasure and inspiration for pupils, parents and staff. They show how art can have a range of effects, from the development of pupils' self-esteem to raising their cultural awareness.

The Hill Primary School is situated in Thurnscoe, Yorkshire, a former mining village which has had high levels of unemployment for some time. The headteacher is determined to use art to raise pupils' levels of self-esteem and recognise successful achievement. Art is planned thoroughly, materials and equipment are prepared impeccably, instructions are clear, and teaching is rigorous and includes both direct instruction and careful judgements of pupils' attainment. The art curriculum is planned in detail, covering each year group. Weekly plans draw on the detailed art policy and identify learning objectives within the National Curriculum programmes of study, as well as extension tasks for the highest attainers. The pupils have a strong interest in the quality of

Examples of artwork from The Hill Primary School, Thurnscoe

their school environment, reflected in the way they treat the buildings and the way they care for the many plants, animals and birds in the school's quadrangle which are regularly used as subject matter for their art work. The headteacher's interest in art and the appointment of an art co-ordinator have steadily lifted the profile of the subject and have led to high quality work.

Although the school buildings are not attractive externally, classrooms are spacious and the environment is rich with stimulus in the form of artefacts, framed prints and good displays of pupils' work.

In a Year 6 lesson, the art activities taking place were inspired by a residential visit to Whitby. The pupils made observed drawings of shells in ink and of pebbles in pencil crayon. Paintings were developed from these drawings, and in turn the paintings were the starting point for embroidery. A scanner, a computer and a printer were used to reproduce the paintings, and the pupils worked into the copies of their paintings with thread. Instructions to the pupils were clear, and high expectations were realised in the way pupils behaved and responded to the task. The teacher's praise was valued all the more because it was reserved for real effort and achievement. The lesson ended with an appraisal of the pupils' work which allowed the teacher to suggest improvements to the whole class. She also involved the children in deciding how and where to display the end products.

The decision to target art as an area of the curriculum through which pupils can experience and appreciate success is making a very positive contribution to the school's ethos.

Not all art co-ordinators start with extensive knowledge of art, but many successful ones develop strategies for improving art in their schools.

At St Peter's CE Primary School in Harrogate, North Yorkshire, the art co-ordinator has devised an art curriculum which is carefully planned to develop both technical art skills and an awareness of a wide range of art forms. An audit of art practice in the school allowed the co-ordinator to identify gaps in provision and to take steps to provide INSET and support for her colleagues. This has given teachers greater confidence in teaching art and has improved standards.

In the shared Key Stage 1 art area, materials and equipment are meticulously organised and labelled, and are placed carefully at the right height and in a logical sequence for collection. The co-ordinator knows how important visual resources are, and has acquired a wide selection of postcards and posters of artists' work. To broaden the range of references, she has bought a reasonably-priced collection of fine specimens of African art from a commercial supplier. These are an invaluable curriculum resource with long-term potential.

References to different art forms start early in this school. In a Year 1 lesson pupils make clay figures based on the Chinese *Terracotta Army* as part of their project on Chinese life and culture. They start by rolling a cylinder of clay, then make oblique cuts into it, pulling out the arms and legs from the cylinder rather than adding them on. The teacher has previously introduced practical techniques of working with clay and established in the pupils' minds a connection between their own work and that of another

Art materials and equipment are well organised and labelled at St Peter's Primary School

A collage of materials created by pupils at St Peter's Primary School

Pupils at St Peter's Primary School working with clay to make figures based on the Chinese *Terracotta Army*

artist or maker. All around them the pupils see other examples of Chinese art: calligraphy, textiles and paintings.

Other Key Stage 1 work is based on a visit the pupils made to an exhibition of textiles by a contemporary textile artist at the Mercer Gallery in Harrogate. The pupils experimented freely with very large, bold textile collages, and abstract shapes and patterns started to appear. If the work had been left at this point, the pupils would have understood little more than how to cut and stick materials down.

The next stage of the lesson was crucial. Each pupil chose a single colour of translucent drawing ink which was brushed over the whole collage. Suddenly the different colours of the collage materials were unified into shades and tints of the one colour, bringing out powerfully the textural qualities of the collages. In this case the teacher's confidence in predicting the effect of adding the ink transformed a routine exercise into an exciting art activity. At the end of the lesson pupils compared their own work with that of the textile artist.

A sound rationale for art is important, but it must be followed through by effective action in the classroom. In this next example, the school's policy documents make it clear that the headteacher, staff and governors all believe firmly that a good arts education makes for well-balanced, confident and socially sensitive pupils, and provides a strong platform of attitudes, skills, knowledge and understanding on which to build their adolescent and adult lives. This is more than mere rhetoric, and is translated into good practice throughout the school. Much depends on the care with which teachers and

their assistants approach the teaching of art. It is important to judge when prescription can be deadening to the imagination; equally there are occasions, as in this example, when pupils learn quickly by being given direct instruction in developing a skill.

At Broughton Junior School in North Lincolnshire the headteacher makes sure that staff have a good knowledge and understanding of art, and that the written guidelines and policies are reflected in practice.

In a Year 6 lesson a group of six pupils made paintings of Ironbridge in Shropshire following a recent visit, using photographs to support the original sketches they made on site. Good quality watercolour paints in boxes with attached palettes were used, as were watercolour brushes (these are not used for any other purpose) and good quality cartridge paper was taped to boards. Pupils worked

Pupils at Broughton Junior School working with watercolours under the guidance of the classroom assistant

with the classroom assistant, who is a watercolour painter in her own right. The pupils received quiet and highly proficient tuition and attained very high standards in this difficult medium. The assistant carefully explained to them what was needed to allow them to make quick progress:

'You paint the darkest part first and leave where you want it to be light.'

'Think of the damp and darkness, drop the paint in and let the water do the job for you...'

'Rest the pillow of the hand on the paper ... just the fingers move ... use a clean brush...'

'You want to wipe out, wipe brush, dab, wipe – now you're getting light and dark – you're getting lumps and bumps in the pasture...'

'Try to demolish that outbuilding in your mind. When you are doing watercolour you are allowed to do that ... it is your impression of the cottage.'

'You've got to do this quickly before that dries...'

'By doing this messy bit you're adding the wear and tear of hundreds of years...'

The pupils responded with deep respect for the medium and the tools used. They worked quietly and with concentrated attention, taking in the instructions and advice. The technique was new to them, but built on ideas and understanding learned in their previous years in the school. The results were good, and they were proud of their achievements.

Schools often make use of the work of artists to meet the requirements of the National Curriculum programmes of study. Much can be learned from the masterpieces of famous artists, but only when pupils are taught to look carefully at the subject matter and techniques involved, and can use this knowledge to support their own work.

At William Tyndale Primary School in Islington, London, a Year 2 class explored the work of Joan Miró, the Spanish painter, looking at the characteristics of his use of shape, colour and composition, painting their own Miró-like portraits and finding out about the artist's life. As part of a school assembly attended and enjoyed by a group of their parents, the class gave a presentation in which they talked about the Miró project, displayed their paintings, showed slides of their own and

Paintings based on the work of Miró by Year 2 pupils at William Tyndale Primary School

Miró's work, and gave some key facts about his life.

Art in this school is well supported by a part-time art teacher who is an artist in her own right. She not only takes classes but is able to work alongside other teachers to help them develop skills in teaching art.

Although the study of famous artists is essential, some schools make very good use of less seminal but equally interesting examples of art, craft and design. For example, contact with a practising artist can transform the approach of teachers and pupils to art.

At Castleview Combined School in Slough an annual arts week included visits to the school by a sculptor whose big wood carvings inspired the pupils when they were given the chance to carve large trunks of timber. The art work in this school effectively promotes the pupils' cultural development through the regular use of examples of the work of a variety of artists and through the use of a fine collection of artefacts such as African masks and Indian dolls.

Art in primary schools in Cheshire has long been well supported by the LEA's art advisory service, which has provided high-quality INSET for teachers and has inspired them to develop art in their own schools. In this next example, a headteacher has been made aware of the importance of art during INSET sessions, and has developed the subject to a high standard in her own school, with the enthusiastic support of the staff.

At Boughton Heath Primary School in Chester, art is a vital part of the school's life, and the work reflects the interest which the headteacher and her staff have taken in developing the subject. Good lesson planning and organisation are seen not only in the choice of activity and the provision of appropriate materials, but in the teachers' decisions about intervention and support for pupils during lessons. The good work begins in the Reception class and goes right through to Year 6.

Pupils in the Reception class are familiar with drawing and painting materials, and are used to working from direct observation. Sitting round tables, they were at work painting clear

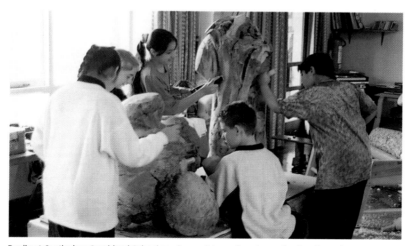

Pupils at Castleview Combined School carving sculptures from huge chunks of wood

glass vases of red tulips. They showed remarkable confidence and competence: washing brushes in the water pot before selecting another colour; dipping them into clean water and then into the small pans of paint in the water colour boxes; looking at the structure of the flowers, then at their work; making marks, stroking the colour onto the paper. The directness of their vision was evident in the colours they selected, and the way in which they attempted to record the actuality of what was in front of them – the tube of the stem, the unexpected turn of a leaf. The class teacher was sensitive to a child's readiness to look more carefully and record more accurately.

The pupils are being helped to acquire the beginnings of a visual language in the same detailed way they are being helped to read and write. They are gradually made familiar with the visual vocabulary of specific elements, including line, tone, colour, texture, shape and form. It is a mark of the success of the teaching that the pupils' use of the visual language conveys meaning.

The lively display of pupils' work in the reception area includes some large line drawings of a bicycle. These vary in perception, but all show evidence of disciplined effort in observation. Some show enough understanding of the mechanism of the bicycle to inform the drawings – the cogs, the chain, the gears. For other pupils it has been a step forward to make bicycle-like marks, thin for the spokes, thick for the frame and some shading on the saddle. These drawings were later developed into small wire sculptures and paper tube constructions which used the skills of cutting, shaping and joining.

With gentle help from their teacher, this same class had earlier conducted an assembly in front of their parents and the rest of the school. They read, they danced, and they showed their drawings in their own sketchbooks of a mother and baby who had visited them recently.

In a Year 2 class practical work was combined with an unusual approach to the introduction of the work of artists. A display about

A display of drawings by the Boughton Heath Primary pupils showing how much they observed and understood bicycles

Gauguin in Tahiti included reproductions of his Tahiti paintings, and a dummy figure of the artist with his suitcase full of sketchbooks, art materials and books about the work of his friend Cezanne. Pupils talked about Gauguin as a person, discussed his motives for moving to Tahiti, then drew in their sketchbooks as the teacher 'dictated' a Gauguin painting. This involved a verbal description of the painting to which the pupils listened intently and drew what they heard described. They were eager to see the painting which they had drawn 'unseen', and gave it their full attention when it was shown to them to compare.

In the same school, Year 5 pupils produced, as a co-operative venture, a large painting in Picasso's style and colours. In previous lessons in this project, the class had examined good quality reproductions of paintings by Picasso and had then drawn four pupils posing with instruments as musicians, a familiar subject in the artist's work. These were carefully enlarged to form a composition which the pupils then took turns to paint. The skills of painting, acquired over the years in the school, were much in evidence. Using acrylic paints, the colours were vibrant and the gestures in the original drawings of the instrumentalists truly expressive. The pupils showed an excellent level of awareness of the artist's work, and were able to express views about their own work using a good number of technical terms.

In Year 6 pupils worked with black markers on large sheets of thin card. Their drawings were based partly on an exhibition of David Hockney's work at the Cheshire LEA's Art Professional Centre in Winsford,

and partly on the pupils' abstract interpretations of maps of the City of Chester. Once the main lines of the picture were complete and the pupils satisfied with the overall composition, they subdivided the voids created by the intersections of the lines with textures and patterns of their choice. Their decisions were made on the basis of which textures and patterns seen in Hockney's work were most pleasing to the eye. The pupils produced good two-dimensional designs and had the confidence to experiment and to revise their work.

Some of the pupils developed their drawings further by selecting an area suitable for enlargement and printing their designs to make simple repeat patterns. Their control of tools was good and, with sensitive guidance from the teacher, they were able to improve the density of the black ink and the 'register' of their prints. It is routine for pupils to organise the materials for painting and printing themselves, and put them away carefully at the end of the lesson.

The pupils' cultural development in relation to the visual arts is exceptional. They have routine first-hand experience of making art, regular experience of looking at art and much talking and writing about art in class. Their work covers a wide range of art, craft and design activities, materials and skills. The school arranges regular contact with working artists, visits to galleries and museums, including the Lady Lever Gallery at Port Sunlight, and makes use of good quality illustrations of works of art, including much from the twentieth century.

Art is extensively displayed around the school and gives an indication of the scope of the work undertaken. Examples include paintings by Year 2 pupils done after studying

Charcoal and pencil drawings of ballet figures by pupils at Boughton Heath Primary School

the work of Mondrian, and charcoal and pencil drawings of figures completed after studying pastel drawings of the ballet by Degas; the practical work is complemented by short biographies of the artists written in the pupils' own words.

Year 3 pupils have been studying Roman artefacts and made well-observed representational drawings of pottery reproductions from a local museum. They have talked about the appearance of Roman pots, and how archaeologists fit small pieces of pottery together to find the shape, size and date. As part of a topic on Ancient Greece, Year 4 pupils portrayed the main characters from the story of 'Perseus the Gorgon Slayer' in batik. They matched their batik work with poems about the characters.

In this school art is strongly influenced by the headteacher who takes on the role of art co-ordinator. She offers her colleagues guidance in planning and in methods and approaches to teaching. Her influence and encouragement are significant factors in the high quality of the pupils' work.

Liaison with The Bishops' CE High School, Chester (see pages 18–20), has been valuable, and both schools have taken part in a joint field centre residential course for primary and secondary pupils.

Art in secondary schools

In Key Stage 3 pupils often make rapid progress from Year 7 to Year 9 in the development of practical skills, and in knowledge and understanding of art. Where the tasks set are challenging and thought-provoking, pupils show a pride in their work; they acquire skills and master techniques and processes which they can control and use to express ideas. Pupils learn how to draw for different purposes. Drawing skills are developed further when pupils go on to evolve compositions and designs in painting, printmaking, collage, textiles and sculpture. Sketchbooks are used to record from observation, to make visual and informal written notes and to generate ideas. The pupils develop skills in working in two and three dimensions, and in using a range of media and techniques, such as paint, collage and clay. They know about the work of artists, enjoy talking about it, and can see its relevance to their own work.

When the pupils talk about their own art their self assessment is realistic, and they show good knowledge of their own capability. The teachers in these schools believe that pupils can and will succeed in art, even when they have had little success in other subjects. Teachers raise the pupils' expectations, and encourage them to look beyond technical accomplishment towards the expression of feeling, meaning and values in art.

At Key Stage 4, the positive characteristics of Key Stage 3 are built on: skills are refined and knowledge is broadened and deepened. The pupils develop the skill of planning their own work; investigating, researching and experimenting with materials to create imaginative and innovative responses. Their individuality is expressed through the accomplished handling of imagery, which often shows original ideas and reflects the influence of other art works. Sketchbooks are used as a medium for recording and gathering source material, and pupils develop their knowledge and understanding of art by talking about their own work, and speculating about the meaning of the work of other artists.

Good post-16 teaching challenges pupils to explore the limits of their practical and intellectual ability, and encourages them to make very rapid progress as they come to realise the creative possibilities of a project. There is an emphasis on pupils' individuality of approach within the framework of well-taught practical and critical skills. Sixth-form pupils can develop drawing skills, often at an exceptional pace, through intensive and challenging teaching; life-drawing can play an important role in this. Pupils gain insights into the styles and conventions of art and enhance their own skills through guided gallery visits and by working with artists-in-residence in their schools. Vocational courses are increasingly giving post-16 pupils scope to learn about and experience the role of the artist, craftsperson and designer in an industrial or business context.

It is clear from what is described here that good work is strongly influenced by the subject expertise and management skills of secondary art teachers. The teachers have a good repertoire of skills, knowledge and understanding in art to support their planning. Their lesson introductions clearly set out objectives which are shared with the pupils, and often include demonstrations of practical techniques. They help pupils to develop critical skills by leading, for example, a session on how to 'interrogate' a famous painting. Well-timed questions and verbal assessments are given to pupils of their work, which is displayed alongside the work of other artists. There are ample opportunities for reflection and critical observation.

Good planning is very strongly associated with high-quality teaching. At its best, lesson planning skilfully predicts how coverage of the curriculum will be affected by staffing, timetabling and resources in the medium to long term. It is sufficiently detailed to ensure consistency and continuity between teachers and years without being prescriptive and inflexible. It specifies and requires the inventive and varied use of formative and summative assessment, both verbal and written, often in response to a good whole-school assessment policy. Pupils know how well they are performing, and they know what they must do to improve. Good planning ensures that teachers monitor and evaluate pupils' progress in particular tasks or projects, and use this information to shape and modify the future curriculum.

The examples quoted here show how different schools in different circumstances are able to meet the challenge of developing or maintaining high standards in art. In some schools the art department has particular issues which arise from its location or catchment area. In this first example a school in Bradford makes good use of the interests and experience of its pupils to enhance the arts, and visual art in particular.

At Bellevue Girls School, Bradford, the very high proportion of Muslim girls brings the scope of culturally acceptable arts practice sharply into focus. The art department has good links with drama through joint involvement in productions for the Bradford Festival, and teachers see this as an informal but important way of maintaining contact with parents, some of whom find more conventional contacts, such as parents evenings, daunting. In the visual arts, there is an emphasis on non-representational work and on textiles in particular. This approach is welcomed by parents and by the pupils, who achieve excellent results in GCSE and A-level art. Many of the sixth-form students go on to art foundation courses in Bradford and then on to textiles degree courses. Work in art draws effectively on the pupils' cultural backgrounds. For example, a piece of homework set for a GCSE textiles group involved finding a new stitch to add to a textile piece. Pupils from Pakistani backgrounds brought in unusual stitches which their mothers and grandmothers had learned in Pakistan.

At The Bishops' CE High School, Chester, a medium-sized comprehensive, the art department is very successful and pupils achieve excellent examination results. The teachers have a very clear view of what their pupils must learn to achieve success in art. Their schemes of work show the content of

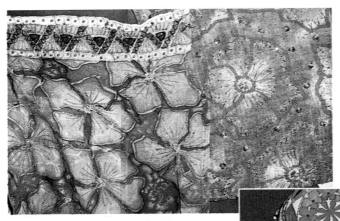

Examples of textile designs by pupils at the Bellevue Girls School

lessons so clearly that a new teacher could fit into the continuing work of the department without difficulty. Sequences of carefully planned activities ensure that the pupils develop their practical, manipulative skills, their understanding of the basic concepts of art and design, and their aesthetic awareness. The high quality of the pupils' homework reflects the commitment which the staff and pupils bring to their work in art and design. In the art lessons teachers maintain firm but kindly discipline.

In a Year 10 lesson, the class used their representational drawings of natural forms as a basis for developing abstract or semi-abstract paintings. The lesson began with a discussion of the work of artists and designers from different historical periods, such as Arcimboldo, Charles Rennie Mackintosh and Georgia O' Keefe. Skilful questioning by the teacher showed that some pupils had good knowledge and understanding of the artists and could use technical terms of art in their comments and explanations. The discussion prompted individuals to find out some answers for themselves from the books and pictures

made available. They had access to a range of good quality materials, and some selected acrylic paints and a mixing palette. The mixing and testing of colours and other essential skills of painting were routine. The high quality of the emerging work owed much to the pupils' careful preparation and supporting homework. The best work revealed a subtle selection and control of colour and sensitive brushwork. The pupils used reference materials very effectively to extend their thinking and their perceptions, and their work showed evidence of personal interpretation.

In another lesson, a Year 11 group worked in the textiles studio which contains displays of textile 'mobiles' and sculptures hanging from the ceiling and moving slightly in the air currents. The scale of the work ranges from miniature pieces of delicate threadwork to large hanging sculptures 6 feet across.

In this lesson the pupils were completing major GCSE projects: there were textile pieces based on the observation of cell and plant structures, of woven and knitted textures and of architectural forms.

A finished mobile by pupils at The Bishops' CE High School

A pupil discusses her design with a teacher at The Bishops' CE High School

The work showed vigour, involving large shapes and strong colours, or, in other pieces, delicacy and fine detail. The pupils dyed their own yarns and planned carefully the 'families' of colours they wished to use. Their textile pieces were examples of good creative art, communicating ideas, feelings and experiences, and at the same time were examples of good craft. The good advice given by the teacher was underpinned by her creative imagination and practical skills, and this encouraged a lively response from the pupils.

All the pupils are given opportunities to use computers in art. Two computers are installed in the department and pupils use them in turn, following a prepared brief. The IT room, with a large network consisting of a server with 20 powerful desktop machines, is next door. The art and IT staff work closely together, and the software used for art and design is fully installed in all the computers.

In a Year 12 lesson a student studying for A-level art had taken a photograph of his small sculpture using a digital camera and loaded it into a computer. Using dedicated software he manipulated the image, and placed it in various landscape locations while greatly increasing the virtual sculpture's size. He skilfully used the computer to delete some features and add others. The landscape drawing and photography which formed the locations for the piece were loaded into the computer using a scanner, and the images were printed in both black and white and colour. The images were good examples of the creative use of a computer. Another student took digital photographs of circuit boards, maps and diagrams which he then superimposed on his landscape paintings. He showed well-developed skills, and the resulting images were successful as art.

At Neston County High School, South Wirral, the quality of teaching and the leadership of the head of department are major factors in the high standards achieved in art. The head of department leads successfully by example. His good teaching and organisation encourage high standards from staff and pupils. The six art teachers share aims and objectives and are clear about the purposes of their work. They discuss and reach agreement on what will be taught and how it will be taught. They know what steps pupils need to take to develop a skill or understand a concept, and they create an approach to work in which ideas are readily stimulated and developed. They understand the need for continuity through the key stages; for example, one of them has written a discussion paper on the nature of progression in the core skills of art from Key Stage 1 to Key Stage 4.

Each member of staff is deployed so that their deep knowledge of art, craft and design, and their experience as practitioners, is shown in their lessons, where they give clear instructions and demonstrations.

Many initiatives taken by the art department raise the pupils' cultural knowledge and awareness. These include the regular employment of artists-in-residence, visits to museums and galleries, and participation by pupils and staff in Cheshire local education authority residential courses in Italy and at Cheshire's Menai Centre in Anglesey.

Work in progress and displays at Neston County High School

The next example illustrates the professional skills of the art teacher: the ability to predict the course of a technical process, anticipate the resourcing needs for a particular lesson, exploit visual sources effectively, use language precisely and develop pupils' powers of imagination.

At Penketh High School in Warrington each teaching space contains excellent displays of current and recent work. There is much observed drawing of good quality, with some outstanding three-dimensional work in card, paper and found materials. Colour is used with great sensitivity. Stress on the use of pattern and ornament has led to work of exceptional quality both on surfaces, such as printed textiles, and in decorated sculpture.

Books and illustrations of native Australian art have provided the source of inspiration and ideas for a Year 9 extended project making drawings, prints, collages and decorative sculptures. Firstly, pupils made line drawings from the illustrations provided, which were then developed into collages and prints. For homework, pupils constructed boxes based on the shapes of the original Australian images of animals, using card and adhesive tape. In school, the boxes were decorated using good quality paints.

The powerful use of imagination is evident in the work. The pupils have imagined the function of the artefacts they are designing. They have imagined how the images they are creating in one medium would look in another. The stimulating ambience of the art rooms, with displays of work of good quality, encourages pupils to use their imagination and produce work of comparable quality. By Year 9, pupils are well used to the process of recalling and

Prints and decorative sculptures developed from native Australian designs at Penketh High School

combining observed images with mental images in order to form new ideas. Overall, the work in this project shows much skill in the pupils' choice of colours. Proficiency in craft, for example in the construction of the boxes, is an integral part of pupils realising their ideas and intentions.

Lesson planning relates well to the overall art and design curriculum, and good learning objectives are set. After a thorough introduction to the class, individual pupils are given advice, and the teaching shows sensitive awareness of each pupil's stage of development and the steps needed to make progress. The quality of the language used by the teachers is a key factor in the success of the lessons. It is not only encouraging, but also precise and illuminating.

The quality of pupils' work on display and in their folders reflects the teachers' command of the subject, and the way in which the

teacher's particular specialisms are exploited. Excellent use has been made of external resources, such as a visit to the Art of Africa exhibition at the Royal Academy of Arts, as well as the department's skilfully selected collection of books and slides.

The art and design curriculum is broad and well-balanced. It includes drawing, which is given major importance, painting, three-dimensional work, printing and textiles. Planning is of very good quality. The head of department has produced policy papers which, after discussion by the team, have led to a framework for the scheme of work. In designing the content of the art and design course, each member of staff proposed individual projects for their own teaching which were discussed at minuted departmental meetings. The exceptional quality of the pupils' work in pattern and ornament, for example, has been enabled by

A Penketh pupil producing high quality pattern and ornament work

the consultative approach to curriculum construction.

Work done in class and for homework is marked regularly, and at the end of each project the staff complete a proforma for each pupil which records achievements and progress. This includes entries for the relevant pieces of homework and space for the parents to sign as having seen the record. At the end of each term, all Year 10 to Year 13 pupils complete a self-assessment record, which includes a list of completed projects and space for pupils' comments and staff response.

Resources are of good quality and include an exceptional collection of books on contemporary artists, which is on open display to encourage browsing. Careful use is made of all materials, including 'waste' such as corrugated card from packing cases. Resources are well selected and represent good value for money.

At Elmhirst School in Barnsley, the new headteacher and the staff have successfully begun to move the school forward. Art has played an important role in giving pupils a powerful sense of achievement.

The highly organised and professional approach taken by the art teachers results in the art department having a very strong identity. Art accommodation is good, with a pleasant and well organised separate block. The first impression on entering the department is of the visual impact of the meticulous displays of paintings, drawings and sculptures. The quality of these displays gives important messages to pupils and visitors about the department's high expectations. The work is varied, but there is one consistent theme: pupils are able to make personal statements and express their feelings and ideas through art in this school.

For example, a Year 11 boy had produced a fine ceramic piece on the theme of 'The journey'. He used well developed skills to make small figures in clay, placed in a tiny stage set. His use of glazes was particularly inventive. He enjoys handling materials, and the teacher has provided a GCSE course which has consistently and methodically encouraged him to explore this interest. Art, and Design and Technology are likely to be his best GCSE grades, and he hopes to go on to a course in building and construction at a local college.

Art is regarded as a 'special' subject in this school. There is scope for pupils of all levels of ability to succeed, and the teachers are particularly good at maintaining the motivation of Year 11 pupils. The head of department gives a strong lead, and staff are expert in the subject, committed to the success of their pupils and know in detail what each of them must do to achieve that success. This close attention to detail encourages pupils to have confidence in their teachers and provides them with powerful motivation right through to the end of their examination courses.

The final example describes a school's very successful use of on-site exhibitions and artist residencies. The effort and entrepreneurial skills currently needed to find funding and to maintain such a programme of exhibitions and residencies should not be underestimated. At present there is no single source of finance, or of artists, which makes this process easy. Although some LEAs and regional arts boards offer the opportunity to buy into residency schemes they do not always provide the time or depth of reciprocal experience between the artist and the school which marks the success of this example.

For many years Abraham Guest High School in Wigan LEA has been committed to bringing its pupils into contact with practising artists, craftspeople and designers, to observe their work and to experience their particular creative processes at first hand. This reflects the innovative accomplishments in Wigan schools of the former art adviser for Wigan in demonstrating the importance of forming connections between pupils' and artists' work. As long ago as 1986 the art and design department restored what had previously been a caretaker's house on the school grounds to create a school gallery, the *Guesthouse*. Local sponsorship, the determined efforts of the teachers in the department, and the commitment of the senior management of the school have managed to maintain this space as a gallery, despite all the growing demands on available space that the school has experienced over the past 10 years.

Since opening, the gallery has been used for up to three exhibitions a year; two are given over to artists' work, usually with an artist in residence, and one to pupils' work. The aims of the gallery set out the benefits for the pupils and the artists and designers. Its aims are:

- to provide pupils with the opportunity to engage directly with the exhibiting artists' work, whenever possible providing workshop experience with the exhibiting artist

- to provide gallery space for artists to promote their own work, maintaining one area in the building as a studio

- to provide other local schools, both primary and secondary, and more recently the community, with the opportunity of sharing this resource

- to display pupils' own work in a gallery situation.

The school remains committed to the LEA's curriculum philosophy of access to the arts for all pupils throughout their time in school. Pupils must take an arts subject at Key Stage 4. The success of the art and design department over many years makes it the most popular choice among the pupils. Over 80 percent of pupils opt for visual arts GCSE courses. There are over 170 pupils in each of Year 10 and Year 11 at present, with a total of 16 groups in each of these years. The *Guesthouse* provides an essential space for the school's annual assessment exhibition for GCSE.

GCSE results are particularly high, with over 90 percent of pupils attaining A–C grades in one of the three courses studied: drawing and painting; textiles; and 3-dimensional studies, in which in 1996 half the candidates gained A* grades.

Year 11 pupils' work produced in conjunction with an artist-in-residence when they were in Year 10, and their GCSE work produced since, illustrates the 'ripple' effect that the involvement with practising artists can have on the development of pupils and on the progress they can make. This effect is enhanced when it is set within a well-planned programme of work; ideas and work stimulated by the artist can be supported, and extended further, once the immediate contact is over.

The artist was resident at the school for a year. She met pupils of all ages to discuss work on exhibition in the gallery and the work she was producing in the studio space. She shared her working processes and the influences on her own development, particularly work by other artists. At the outset of the residency the art and design department followed its customary practice of using a curriculum development day to explore the artist's own work and thinking in

some depth; to discuss strategies for joint teaching; and to plan the continuing project work which would develop from the artist's workshops with pupils.

Workshops focused on the theme of movement and the interplay of surface and texture. Pupils saw how the artist reacted to this interplay, and how her observations stimulated new ideas and new directions as her work progressed.

Stemming from these initial sessions, teachers developed projects exploring the quality of surface and texture in clay. Pupils produced their own relief surfaces, later turning the 'flat' clay surfaces into rolled sculptures of often quite outstanding quality.

Other work focused on juxtapositions and interactions of materials and textures in developing surfaces from paper and pulp.

Displays of sculptures at Abraham Guest High School

The notion of joining and combining pieces was introduced, stimulating thinking about the concept of 'books', and the book as container of meaning or a record of events. In their resulting work each pupil interpreted the central theme, exploring different, and in many case highly inventive and imaginative, outcomes in the form of 'books' or 'boxes'.

The range and individuality of the work and the level of exploration in the finished pieces demonstrates not only the powerful stimulus provided by the artist, but also the quality of the art course itself. The degree of maturity the pupils had already developed for their age gave them the confidence to respond positively and creatively to opportunities for exploration and experimentation, and the ability to understand and work with concepts of art – often quite abstract in nature – which were the stimulus for the artist's own work.

Residencies can build upon the building bricks of artistic ability and understanding that pupils already have; they can and do accelerate learning, but the extent of progress that pupils make and the depth of the experience possible is directly linked to the base they start from and the quality of education they have received.

The 'ripple' effect, and the key interrelationship between the specific stimulus of the artist and the pupils' continuing art education, was further illustrated in the work that many pupils had produced in the following year and were now finalising for their GCSE exhibition. For example, during the drawing sessions on movement led by the artist, one pupil very successfully captured in a single life-size drawing a sequence of actions over time. Since then her teacher had guided her to

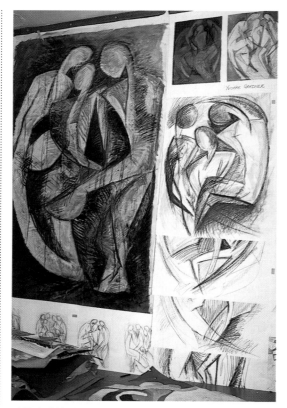

Highly individual work by a pupil at Abraham Guest High School that has drawn on the kind of influences that shaped some of Picasso's work

associated work by other artists, including the Futurists, Marcel Duchamp's *Nude Descending Stairs*, and to early Cubist work. While studying the influences of African art on the development of Western art following a visit to Liverpool museum she became aware of these particular influences on Picasso's early work. Her final painting, on a similarly dramatic scale to the original drawing, reflected this train of influences; interpreting the influences in a mature and individual way, which ensured that the style and content of the painting was very much her own, rather than simply pastiche or an emulation of another artist's style.

In other examples the ideas stimulated by the 3-dimensional structures and containers had developed into some highly individual sculptural pieces combining ideas of structure and surface in exciting and inventive ways. The high level of visual research and the investigation of other contemporary artists and sculptors expected by teachers had built on the original stimulus, producing a quality of work well above that normally expected of pupils studying GCSE.

This example shows a number key factors which help to ensure the success of a partnership between an artist and and a school.

- A committed senior management, with a vision of the curriculum, wishing to provide an experience of the arts to all pupils, and the commitment to resourcing that provision.

- An approach to residencies which recognises that, for the experience to have a significant effect, there has to be sufficient time for pupils to get to know the work of the artist and their working process; and sufficient depth to the experience for pupils' own imagination and creativity to be fired up.

- A respect for the artist which acknowledges them as more than just a temporary resource and acknowledges their professional and creative needs as an equal partner.

- A very well managed department which:

- has a clear vision of the subject, high expectations of pupils, combined with a high level of professional knowledge and understanding of the subject

- sets out to encourage individual development rather than just the mastery of specific skills

- has a clear and well structured programme that introduces pupils to the work of other artists, craftspersons and designers through all available resources, including exhibitions, loaned works and extracurricular visits

- encourages pupils to explore the influences that affect the work of other artists and which might similarly influence their own.

3 Dance

Gordon Clay HMI

SPECIALIST ADVISER FOR PHYSICAL EDUCATION

I N schools, dance has a place in the National Curriculum as one of the six required areas of activity in the Physical Education Order (DFE 1995). It is compulsory for all pupils during Key Stages 1 and 2. Its place in Key Stage 3 is optional, though dance or gymnastics – the areas of physical activity which focus exclusively on learning to manage the body – must be included for at least a half unit. Dance may be a chosen area of activity at Key Stage 4 and has examination syllabuses at GCSE, AS- and A-level. In some secondary schools dance is not taught by the teachers in the PE department, or through the physical education curriculum, but in an 'expressive' or 'creative arts' department. The place of dance, as part of physical education or as an art form in its own right, has been debated within education over many years. Where dance is taught within the curriculum in schools is less important than that it is taught to a high standard by knowledgeable teachers guided by a well-planned scheme of work that provides continuity and progression within and across key stages.

This chapter shows how dance can make an important contribution to education and illustrates some characteristics of good work in schools. Dance in education not only contributes to the physical development of pupils, it also promotes the development of artistic and aesthetic qualities, and the acquiring of control, co-ordination and versatility in the use of the body.

Dance is a discipline that requires pupils to compose and to explore ideas, improvise solutions to problems, select the most appropriate actions and shape movements into dance phrases and motifs, and practise and refine their work. This is preparation for controlled performance which combines technical competence and appropriately rehearsed interpretation of a theme. Being able to comment critically on a finished dance or work in progress requires observation and analytical skills, knowledge of appropriate criteria, and understanding of the different styles and forms of dance. This three-part process of composing, performing and appraising is the most important feature of the National Curriculum in dance, and in all aspects of physical education. It is a single interrelated cycle, rather than three individual strands, and underpins the development of knowledge, understanding and physical skills in dance. As pupils move from being able to make up and dance short, simple phrases, about which they make comment at an early age, to highly polished performances of elaborate dances based on sophisticated themes at GCSE level, this process remains central.

Children – with their tendency to run, skip, hop, jump and turn in their play – dance spontaneously and freely from a young age. Inspection findings show that dance is well established in most primary schools. Here, the early exuberant physical activity is gradually refined, and given structure and purpose, in the making of simple dance phrases in reception classes. By the end of Key Stage 2, many pupils work effectively in groups to compose and perform elaborate and well-developed dances from a wide range of stimuli and themes, and are able to make judgements about their own work and that of others. At all stages dance can link well with other subjects and make a substantial contribution to the pupils' spiritual, moral, social and cultural development. Much of the work in dance depends on working together effectively in groups, and success provides enjoyment, as well as contributing to improved self-esteem and self-confidence.

Inspection also shows, however, that dance is not taught continuously to all pupils throughout the primary years or to the majority of pupils in secondary schools. Although dance is well established in primary schools, often the continuity of the work is broken, with consequent loss of progression in attainment, because some class teachers lack the confidence to teach dance. There is a substantial need for in-service training for these primary teachers. In secondary schools a small proportion of teachers are dance specialists and almost all specialist physical education teachers have had some training in the teaching of dance. However, many of the latter group are more inclined to the teaching of games or other areas of activity. As a result, they often make curriculum choices on behalf of pupils that are governed more by the teachers' expertise than an accurate reflection of a balanced curriculum for the young people in their charge. Dance is provided for the majority of girls at some stage in Key Stage 3, but is less frequently available for boys. It is most often offered within the physical education department and, in those schools where dance is taught, it is frequently taught well and attainment levels are high. Where dance is offered as an examination subject at Key Stage 4 and post-16, GCSE, AS and A-level examinations attract relatively small numbers of well-motivated students and results are often good when compared to other subjects in the same school.

Many primary and secondary pupils perform their dances in lessons, in assemblies and more widely for parents and others within the school. A large number are involved in public performances at the growing number of dance events and festivals around the country and, indeed, internationally. These can be memorable occasions which have a lasting effect on pupils. After one such local event, a pupil – from a secondary school in which a high number of pupils were not achieving the levels expected of their age and in an area of serious social and economic deprivation – sent a card to her teacher which simply said, 'Thanks. This is the best thing that ever happened in my life.' In recent years there has been a rapid development in professional dance, which has been given greater exposure on television and has led to an increasing number of small dance companies, offering a wide range of styles, working with schools. This extends the dance experience of pupils and many more now see live dance in their school hall or the local theatre, and have the opportunity to work with professional dancers in workshop classes. These activities give a clear sense of direction to pupils' own work, and help them raise their expectations concerning standards.

Inspection indicates that where standards of attainment are high and progress is being made consistently, pupils:

- move with increasing control and clarity of intention

- explore and express moods and feelings in dance, and are sensitive to sound or music accompaniment or stimulus

- have good sense of rhythm, body tension and spatial awareness

- use varying speeds of action and stillness to good effect

- work alone, in pairs and groups with confidence

- develop understanding and use in context of body actions such as travelling and stopping, turning and spinning, jumping and landing, gestures and stillness, and eventually lifting and falling

- develop more extended dance phrases and motifs with increasingly complex forms

- create dances in different styles using character and narrative as starting points

- perform dances taught by the teacher

- are able to comment critically on their own work and that of others.

Not all lessons contain each of these features and not all pupils in all classes have high standards of attainment. However, in the better lessons attainment usually shows a number of these features in combination depending on the age and stage of development of the pupils.

This was written about pupils at Lucas Vale Primary School in Lewisham and it shows both high levels of achievement and clear progress from reception to the end of Key Stage 2.

By the age of five pupils know the names of basic actions and can identify the movements from a video snippet of Nureyev. Pupils perform running actions on feet followed by stretching, turning and closing movements. They can make their own response to a task, such as different ways of rolling and turning, and can remember and repeat the same movements in the correct sequence. Pupils use the space very well and stretch using their whole body. They can count for four as they run for four counts, stretch for four counts and close for four counts. Pupils listen to music well and know when to begin moving. They repeat their own movement phrase and work with a partner to extend the dance. They know and can describe who is running and who is holding still.

By the end of Key Stage 2 pupils can observe and discuss the dance movements seen in a video of *Swan Lake*. They use appropriate language such as *repetition*, *isolation* and *focus*. They can identify and describe the focal point for the dancers. Pupils learn, remember and perform a Russian dance that involves taught steps and uses motifs. They compose an alternative dance phrase for use in the Russian dance. Pupils give good evaluative comments and suggest ways to improve the dance such as 'maintain the focus throughout' and 'stretch and hold the balance shape very still.'

Key Stage 2 pupils at Stamford Park Junior School, Trafford, also made clear progress and showed good understanding in their work as it developed over four years.

Pupils in Year 3 worked accurately and repeated their own chosen movement with a degree of precision. They had good awareness of shape and body tension and of timing and rhythm. Their phrasing was well developed. They offered critical comment on the work of other pupils. By Year 4, pupils also thought about the use of shape in their work and were producing an interesting range of travelling patterns. They were prepared to be inventive and were able to recall and repeat motifs and phrases fairly accurately and with control. Their detailed observation of movement and attentive listening to music was a strong feature of their work. They were developing the ability to present their work effectively, taking account of how the dance would look to an audience at the front.

The pupils in Years 5 and 6 showed clear development of their work and were building on that of earlier years. Some pupils in both years had very good or outstanding ability. The Year 5 pupils showed sensitive interpretation of the music and confidently built fluent movement patterns. Good movement quality contrasts were used with understanding and transitions between phrases were performed skilfully. They had a good sense of rhythm. They had clear body shape and good tension qualities. They were able to work on their created ideas and refinements. The Year 6 pupils had many of these characteristics and produced clear and precise performances with accurate reproduction of movement. They had good memories for movement and showed good understanding and knowledge of the process of building a dance. The control of the dynamics and spatial qualities were good. They worked very well in pairs, and their attainment was high.

Creating dances is a central activity in classes, but learning to refine dances, rehearse for precision and perform dances for an audience of peers in class, for the whole school – perhaps in an assembly – or a wider audience beyond school introduces a powerful motivation for pupils. This raises standards, sharpens attention to detail and demands close attention to accuracy of the movement. Many pupils at the Ash Green County Primary School in Staffordshire create excellent dances and have performance experience and skills beyond their years.

During the inspection visit pupils showed a range of dances in contrasting styles.

There were dances by pupils from Years 3, 4, 5 and 6. Year 3 performed a comic dance entitled 'Singing in the Rain' and a second one called 'A Day Trip to Bangor'. Year 4 pupils handled a more complex theme based on the First World War which sharply contrasted two dance styles: the first was a seaside scene at the beginning of the war and the second was a dance about life in the trenches. Year 4 later produced contrasting humorous dances about shoes, feet and walking entitled 'The Monster Plod'. Year 5 showed a dance entitled 'Jitterbug' in a 1920s style and the Year 6 group danced a poignant performance based on an environmental project on rain forests entitled 'Tall Trees'.

Overall the dance quality was remarkable and well above national standards at this key stage. There was clear evidence of progression and development through the ages. A wide range of stimuli had been used, including well-chosen music, and carefully selected poetry. The sound quality to accompany the work was very high. The choice of both stimuli and accompaniment was well handled and entirely appropriate.

The range of dance styles was interestingly wide. Every dance included contrast and pupils were skilful, even at an early age, in motif development. All the dances had a clear thematic base and communicated well the intended meanings. The pupils had good stage presence and well co-ordinated bodily control. They were clear where their audience was when they were performing and were prepared to hold the endings throughout the applause. Some of the performers at all ages were clearly very talented.

The dance work reveals a very positive attitude towards the subject throughout the school. The youngest pupils take part with great enthusiasm and delight and this is retained right through the junior school. It is quite clear that the involvement in dance makes a significant contribution to both behaviour and quality of relationships in the school and makes a significant contribution to other aspects of pupils' personal development. And:

> … the school is invited to many national conferences and festivals. The pupils are used to performing in a variety of significant venues such as the Albert Hall, the Royal Festival Hall, Birmingham and other venues in England. Many pupils have also performed in Germany and will perform this summer in Finland.

Many of these pupils go on to join the dance performance group 'Ziggy', which has met in the school voluntarily on Sundays for the past 17 years and is made up of former pupils. Over the years, the changing membership of 'Ziggy' have made tours to Bali, America and Germany. These are significant events that impact positively on the lives of the young people.

Clearly, not all primary schools achieve the standards described above. Skilful teachers at Key Stage 3 overcome this difficulty in a variety of ways. At the Ellen Wilkinson High School in Manchester dynamic and strongly-led teaching in the early stages gives pupils the confidence to try their own ideas. Their work shows many good qualities and the dance activity is much valued by the senior management in the school.

This extract indicates how much progress was made in the early stages.

The teacher often takes the lead in the lessons and provides plenty of ideas from which the pupils can build their own contributions. This gives them the security to try out new action patterns and short phrases of linked movements which are later developed, with the teacher's help, into more complex and abstract motifs.

As a result, in Year 7 and Year 8 pupils show an ability to create ideas well and quickly, and to repeat phrases clearly and accurately. They all have a good sense of rhythm and have developed a good memory of completed dance phrases and motifs.

They are able to produce clear well-controlled movement patterns. The youngest pupils are beginning to develop an initially mimed action into an abstract motif and the Year 8 pupils are able to handle the notion of motif development with some confidence. The older pupils produce flowing improvisation which is based on good knowledge and understanding gained from outstanding teaching. They understand and can use technical language and are aware of the processes of building a dance. Their excellent bodily control includes falling techniques.

Pupils practising dance movement at the Ellen Wilkinson High School

Pupils at Davison CE High School working on a cross-cultural theme

The Davison CE High School for Girls in West Sussex receives pupils in Year 8. Again, excellent and demanding teaching sets the tone and pupils rapidly attain high standards and make very good progress in their two years in Key Stage 3.

The attainment in dance is well above average. Pupils in Year 8 rapidly settle into dance as an activity and attain highly. The youngest girls have good body awareness of line and tension in particular. They clearly understand relationships in dance and many are developing good fluency in linking movement into a dance phrase. They respond imaginatively to tasks and to new ideas. By Year 9 the girls are giving every indication of a much more extensive previous background than they have actually had. They learn at speed and have developed poise and elegance in their movement, which is controlled and fluent.

They are inventive and prepared to experiment, select and refine to achieve very good quality sequences in groups. They plan, perform and evaluate both their own work and that of others and learn from practice and repetition.

A feature of the work in the school is the clear and rapid progress pupils make in developing dance motifs into dramatic, meaningful dance from an early stage. By Year 9 pupils have made good progress in the development of the dance phrases in groups. They are beginning to bring previous experience, knowledge and understanding to bear and are able to work at good speed. By this stage their knowledge, understanding and skills are probably better than most Year 9 pupils with a more extensive background.

This Key Stage 3 learning at Davison lays the foundation for examination work at Key Stage 4.

The progress of the GCSE group is excellent. The new elements of the compulsory GCSE study piece are learned at considerable pace and quickly transposed from body action into dance. The new choreographic devices introduced to the session are quickly absorbed into their creative work. This is impressive learning.

The BRIT Performing Arts and Technology School in Croydon takes its youngest pupils at Key Stage 4. Pupils are committed to the performing arts and many go on to seek vocational professional training in their chosen field. In an extended 29-hour taught week, pupils follow a full National Curriculum and almost a third of pupils take six hours a week of dance as a major performing arts option at Key Stage 4. Here, too, very good teaching and high expectations result in high standards.

Levels of attainment are very high. The work in Year 10 is of exceptional quality with the major option students. Pupils have very good knowledge and understanding of movement and are able to apply their understanding in context in the creation and performance of individual, pair, small group and large group dances. They are capable of sharing ideas freely and are able to develop their work. They learn at considerable speed and have excellent movement memory. They produce highly creative responses and are able to repeat with accuracy. They make confident contributions to creative work. Almost all have good body awareness and acute appreciation of line, shape and rhythm.

There was evidence of progress in all sessions seen. This was usually related to the further development of work started in an earlier session, but it is quite clear that pupils are able to learn quickly and develop their work with confidence. They show evidence of being able to take on new ideas and to incorporate them into existing work to good effect. The pupils tackle a wide range of dance styles and techniques during their courses and for the most part appear to be able to master them with confidence. The examination results at GCSE and post-16 are exceptionally good.

Examinations in dance at GCSE and A-level make considerable demands on pupils and the award of high grades demands, among a range of other characteristics, technical skill in performance, good knowledge and understanding of movement and of choreographic principles. This could be demonstrated in many ways and from many sources, but notes on this lesson at the Davison CE High School capture many positive qualities in candidates at GCSE examination level.

Girls are technically very strong – precise, accurate, rhythmically sound. Well performed GCSE technical study. Duo compositions of very high standard – compositionally and technically – danced with skill and sensitivity. Intelligent and highly creative choreography that reflects good knowledge and understanding of the process, combined with interpretation ability. Able to copy and learn the new technical study at considerable speed. Fluent and controlled movement for most of the class – about 80 per cent will be graded A or A* at GCSE.

Excellent progress in the GCSE compulsory study which was quickly transposed from body action into dance. New choreographic devices introduced and quickly absorbed into their work. Impressive learning.

Pupils are fully committed to the demanding work. Prepared to mark and repeat frequently to ensure precision in the study. Confident in the duo performances and in other aspects of the work. Cooperative and hard working. Good relationships with each other and the teacher. Highly disciplined approach to the work.

The high quality work described so far depended, without exception, on good teaching. Many of the most effective primary teachers seen in this good practice survey have had some initial dance training or have gained knowledge and expertise through in-service courses. All the most effective secondary teachers are well qualified and have either specialised in dance within a physical education course or trained as a dance specialist. The successful teachers are confident, are clear about their teaching objectives and what they want pupils to learn, and choose their teaching themes, stimuli and materials with care.

This extract from the inspection note of the work at Beauchamp Middle School in Bedfordshire focuses on good planning, sharing clear objectives with pupils and setting high expectations.

The teachers have very good subject knowledge and experience of teaching dance. Enthusiasm is communicated to pupils and is reflected in their very positive response. Lessons are very well planned with clear lesson objectives which are shared with pupils. Throughout lessons and club activities pupils are constantly challenged to improve the quality, choreographic composition, expression and accuracy of their work.

Pupils at Beauchamp Middle School

Similarly high expectations were seen at the Linton Village College in Cambridgeshire where:

> … teaching demands attention to detail on the part of pupils and a 'professional' approach to the work. There are high expectations of even the youngest pupils and the challenge is maintained throughout the school. Good links are made with other arts subjects and the pupils understand that they share ways of working with drama, music and visual arts.

The importance of consistent routines and a clear structure in giving pupils the security they need as the basis for good work in dance is shown at the Park Community School in Havant, Hampshire.

> Routines surrounding lessons are well established and firmly enforced. This gives less well-motivated pupils a clear framework and sets an atmosphere in which they can learn. Lessons start with a reminder of what pupils did last week. This includes questions. All lessons include a warm-up and concluding activity. GCSE groups have a rigorous warm-up which includes good body training as well as preparation for the lesson.

In dance a wide range of teaching styles and approaches are used. In an excellent session with a mixed GCSE class at the Ellen Wilkinson High School, Manchester, the dance teacher directed the work closely at first before using a range of other strategies to allow the work to develop.

> She taught the warm-up and body training parts of the lesson and also taught the GCSE directed study from the front with considerable focus on detail and precision. Pupils then had to work in pairs, and later in groups. They repeated and analysed each other's movements, observing with care and commenting freely and intelligently on how to improve it. They later used video to correct problems and check progress.

The same teacher planned for improvisation and creative work related to 'the circus' with a Year 8 class. She had prepared 'exciting and stimulating teaching material' and adopted 'a demanding teaching style with excellent use of voice, clear structure and lesson development' and allowed 'pupils to choose a sound accompaniment for their work'. There was much carefully aimed praise and ample opportunity for pupils to find solutions for themselves in their compositions, to refine their performance and appraise the work as it developed.

Acute observation of movement and the well-judged timing of intervention in both repetition and creative work are essential skills in teaching dance. Creative work needs time for the experimenting with ideas, the testing of alternatives, the refining of skills and the practice or rehearsal of the finished piece. Well-honed skills of observation and intervention allow helpful, critical feedback to be given to pupils as they work, without destroying their contributions. Pupils learn a technical vocabulary that they can use when commenting on the work of others.

Many teachers used imaginative resources to stimulate creative dance responses. Video of professional dance work was frequently used to good effect and, on occasions, good links were made with other areas of the arts or the wider curriculum. Simple costume, background information, pictures and sound patterns all featured fairly regularly in good lessons. A class of Year 8 girls at Davison CE High School were working on a moving and highly creative dance based on a World War I poem and a projected image on the back wall.

The teacher provided a good role model in leading a thorough warm-up with focus on accurate repetitions of stepping, swinging and stretching phrases; this was an effective body training part of the lesson. Pair activity – working on supported balance, counter balance and focused relationships – developed into a dance motif. The stimulating material of a war poem (*The Fusiliers* by Robert Graves) was sensitively presented and accompanied by an OHP picture projection on the wall. The lesson's clear objectives unfolded progressively and helped the girls to make good progress in skill, knowledge and understanding. The teacher intervened unobtrusively to ensure that the process of planning, performing and evaluating was underpinning the pupils' own work. There were opportunities to watch the work of others. A sensible pace was maintained throughout – no slacking but not over-hurried either.

Where the work was stimulating and challenging, class management was always easy for teachers and in the better lessons seen there was little time for misbehaviour.

Planning for continuity of experience and progression in learning and attainment is difficult in dance. In primary schools much depends on the knowledge and confidence of the individual class teachers to take learning forward from the previous year. In too many schools the experience is intermittent at best and it is very rare to find pupils who have had continuous experience of dance throughout Key Stage 1 and Key Stage 2. The influence of the headteacher and the subject co-ordinator is the factor in success in primary schools. This describes the provision at Stamford Park Junior School in Trafford.

The planning for the dance curriculum is very well organised at school level. Pupils achieve beyond the end of key stage description for Key Stage 2. The curriculum provides equal access for all pupils.

There are no teachers with formal dance qualifications. However, the PE co-ordinator is the experienced deputy headteacher; the dance co-ordinator (who works to the PE co-ordinator) is a dance enthusiast. All teachers teach dance to their own classes. The dance co-ordinator is the most significant contributor to the development of dance; she helps with planning and has been responsible for the development of resource packs and other materials for use by other teachers. The planning for dance teaching as a whole in the school is strong and this helps to lift the quality and consistency of the work. Assessment is effective and on-going and informs curricular planning.

A major factor in the curriculum organisation and planning for the subject is that dance occurs in the context of a much broader approach to the arts and aesthetic development generally. The headteacher is totally committed to good arts education. An annual school production is included in the term's planning for the curriculum. Every pupil in the school takes part and each class is responsible for developing a scene for the production based on work in the planned curriculum. The production is an entirely collaborative event that involves all the staff and pupils, and also many parents and outsiders.

The rehearsals for this major production occur in lesson time, since they are curriculum-related. There are possibilities of additional specific rehearsals at lunchtime or during club time. The production has elements of dance, drama and music linked together by singing. Costumes are made either in school or with the help of parents. The entire production is written in the school itself; commercially created songs and productions are never used.

In this school dance lies within the physical education programme and the 40-minute dance lessons alternate with gymnastics on a termly cycle throughout the school. Shorter periods of time in blocks of fewer lessons rarely provide the progression in knowledge, understanding and skill to enable pupils to achieve highly or to learn in depth. Where dance finds its place in physical education departments in secondary schools, the short block of lessons is often the norm and as few as six or seven lessons per year, limited to Years 7 and 8, are planned in some cases. This bleak picture is not necessarily improved by dance's location in an Expressive or Performing Arts faculty where short cycles of music, dance and drama result in broken experience. Some schools give more generous time allowances such as Ellen Wilkinson High School.

For pupils at Ellen Wilkinson High School dance is a part of the expressive arts curriculum

In Year 7 pupils have one 50-minute lesson every week; in Year 8 and Year 9 they have two 50-minute periods per week on a half-termly carousel arrangement with music and drama. The GCSE groups in Years 10 and 11 have a 100-minute lesson plus a 50-minute lesson per week. There is equality of access and opportunity for all pupils and the boys and girls follow the same dance course to Year 9; all have the chance to take a GCSE course in Years 10 and 11. The programme is well planned to provide effective continuity of learning and progression in attainment throughout the school. This lays a strong base for those who wish to pursue dance in the later years. Pupils are regularly assessed in dance as part of the physical education assessment.

And the Dartford Grammar School for Girls also gives dance a firm place in the curriculum.

The dance curriculum in school promotes high standards. It is planned in considerable detail. Overall, during the key stage dance is given about a quarter of the time available for physical education. In Key Stage 4 all girls follow a single 50-minute period of dance throughout Year 10. In addition, a percentage of the pupils opt for dance at GCSE. At post-16 small numbers of pupils opt to follow A-level or AS-level courses in dance.

Only a small minority of schools nationally enter pupils for GCSE and post-16 examinations. However, where dance is strong in the school, GCSE classes of more than 20 students were seen. A-level classes are usually very small.

In most of the schools visited for the survey, the structured learning in the curriculum was greatly enhanced by a wide range of extracurricular opportunities. These take many forms: regular lunchtime, after-school or weekend open-access clubs, rehearsals for performances, youth groups, workshops with visiting dance artists or specialist technique teachers, residency master classes. There is no set pattern. Some are for the enjoyment of dance only; others have a more serious intent. Discussion with the youth group 'Ziggy', meeting at the Ash Green Primary School, indicated that:

… very few of them would be interested in going on to a vocational career in dance (although a few do) and most of them take part for pleasure and the social opportunity it provides. They also mention the dance teacher with particular affection and acknowledge the immense impact she has had on their personal lives through the activity of dance.

But at the Lucas Vale Primary School:

Dance club is available for any pupils from Years 4, 5 or 6. Fifty-six pupils attend regularly throughout the year and work for two years on a production that brings together many strands of experience for pupils, in particular literature, art, dance, science and technology. Common to all these is the need for discipline and a commitment to high standards, whether it is timing in dance, determining the best materials for a mask or uncovering the layers of a story. Pupils learn a complex and explicit body of knowledge.

And at Ellen Wilkinson High School:

There are plenty of opportunities for participation in extracurricular activity. Numbers vary according to different performance activities but usually average around 20 per session. The school always has a production in dance in mind. In this academic year the school has used, in curriculum time and in the extracurricular programme, VTOL dance company, Phoenix Dance Company, Stark Dancers, English National Ballet, RJC Dance Company (Reggae, Jazz and Contemporary) and also has links with Manchester Youth Dance Group and the School Youth Dance Group. The School Youth Dance Group is a group of more than 20 pupils or former pupils who come to school twice a week to take part in performance activity.

While at Hextable School, Kent:

Provision for extracurricular activities in dance is excellent, with dance clubs for all year groups which are well attended. The sixth form organises its own Hextable Dance Company, which successfully organises its own dance event from the choreography to the publicity and takes the event into the local feeder schools. This year the pupils are organising their own production of *Grease*. The school organises an Arts Festival that runs for three weeks. This event covers a wide range of dance styles and experience. The programme includes an arts week, a social and folk dance week, a dance and disability week, an art and the community event and a week for primary school pupils in Years 5, 6 and 7.

Pupils at Ellen Wilkinson High School rehearsing one of their dance productions

It can easily be seen that the rich provision made in some schools spills over into the provision for the wider community. Some events are significant though small in scale, such as at the Trinity CE High School, Manchester, which, among other wide-ranging dance activities, provides dance performance as part of the Eucharist in the church or the cathedral.

Others are highly complex, such as the Hextable School programme, where the Community Arts Centre provides courses throughout the year in a wide range of art events. The co-ordinator has a dual role of dance co-ordination within the school combined with organisation of the Community Arts Centre. The programme includes a weekly choreographic and technique class in the evening, as well as the chance to try line dancing, tap, Latin American styles of dance, and an Annual Festival which offers students the chance to be part of new works choreographed by members of the Jiving Lindy Hoppers, the Royal Ballet and the Rambert Dance Company.

The Arts Festival is organised and held at Hextable School and links a wide range of local organisations and events including: the Keep Fit Association; the Dance Centre catering for ballet, tap, modern, jazz, singing, drama, boys' specialisation classes; folk/social dance including Latin American, Bhangra and Giddha, Irish dancing, English folk, Morris dance, Scottish sword dance, South American dancers, barn dance, ballroom dance, line dance and rock 'n' roll; Kent County Council's Youth and Community Dance Group; and the Swing Stars.

As part of Hextable Dance Festival, Artability presented a week exploring dance and disability. This included: creative dance and improvisation with Eckhar Thiemann and percussionist Neville Murray and students from Goldsmith's College, University of London; the Magpie Dance Company, an integrated dance company involving people with and without learning disability; and Sarah Scott, a deaf artist who uses sign-song with movement to create language. Students from the Certificate in Music Workshop Skills course run by Goldsmith's College provided live music throughout the week.

Arts for 9–12s included a week of creative workshops with the Jiving Lindy Hoppers, the Royal Ballet and the Rambert Dance Company.

As the recent Arts Council of England publication *Arts Organisations and their Education Programmes* (ACE 1997) shows, the role of professional dancers in schools continues to grow strongly. The work of these visiting artists is highly valued in schools where dance teaching is effective and well-established. It provides considerable stimulation for those involved and often injects a new level of motivation to work hard and to achieve highly. Professional dancers provide role models of bodily skill and performance towards which pupils can aspire, and work in classes often gives new insights into choreographic structures and principles that can later be applied in their own creative work. These experiences also have the potential to enhance observation and critical skills.

It is clear from the examples of good practice seen during the survey that the best provision in schools gives continuous experience and a steady progression in the development of knowledge, understanding and skill in dance. This is enhanced by extracurricular work in school and is linked directly to wider community provision in an area. The best schools lay the foundation for life-long learning and enjoyment in dance.

4 Drama

John Hertrich HMI

SPECIALIST ADVISER FOR ENGLISH

THE place of drama in the curriculum rests on its inclusion in all three of the Attainment Targets for English in the National Curriculum (DFE 1995). For example, in Attainment Target 1 (Speaking and Listening) at Key Stage 1 'pupils should be encouraged to participate in drama activities, improvisation and performances of varying kinds, using language appropriate to a role or situation. They should be given opportunities to respond to drama they have watched, as well as that in which they have participated.' In Attainment Target 3 (Writing) at Key Stages 3 and 4, in order to develop their ability to write scripts and dialogue, pupils should be encouraged to:

- use their experience of reading, performing and watching plays
- develop their use of dialogue to convey character.

In addition, drama has a long history as a popular practical artistic subject in its own right. It is also a powerful vehicle for work in a range of subjects; and it contributes to pupils' personal, social, moral and spiritual development. Pupils may experience drama in a wider sense – the pageantry, ritual and moving speeches which play an important part on occasions of national or spiritual significance, such as the funeral of Diana, Princess of Wales. Most children first encounter drama through their own early play and they continue to experience it almost every time they watch television. For many pupils, sharing a performance with peers, family or another audience is a memorable and enjoyable experience. Similarly, a visit to the theatre or working with professional actors in school can help pupils explore the imaginative act that lies at the heart of all drama.

At its best drama in schools gains from such multi-faceted provision. OFSTED's inspection findings (Hertrich 1997) show that drama is popular with pupils, that standards are highest in Key Stages 1 and 4 and that the best teaching occurs in the latter, where the subject is most likely to be taught by staff with relevant qualifications or extensive experience of teaching drama. It is clear that high standards in drama are characterised by the ability of pupils to:

- take on and sustain convincingly one or a number of roles

- explore how individuals or groups in a specific situation behave: handling conflict; trying out a number of solutions to a problem; or using dramatic play as a way of testing relationships and making sense of the world

- deepen their understanding: of themselves and others, of issues or of texts

- improve their communication and movement skills

- learn about and use the concepts which underpin drama: fiction, character, plot, setting, symbols and dramatic conventions, including those of time, space and language

- acquire specific techniques, such as improvisation, simulation[1], freeze-frame[2], tableaux[3], thought-tracking[4], forum theatre[5] and hot-seating[6]

- make effective use of available resources and spaces

- develop a critical approach to their own drama and to performance by others, whether in the theatre, on television or in other settings.

Drama always involves more than one person; even a soliloquy is delivered to an audience.

Good drama contributes to pupils developing important attitudes and values which relate to the fundamental aims of schools: self-esteem, self-confidence, a willingness to co-operate, mutual understanding, and – not least – enjoyment.

For all this to happen, schools need to have a clear rationale which spells out pupils' progress in drama as they move through the school, and the levels of attainment expected at each stage. Like other arts subjects, drama depends upon teachers having the necessary expertise, a curriculum which ensures that pupils have access to drama in the classroom and, if possible, as an extracurricular activity, and sufficient resources – in the case of drama, at least a designated space. There are considerable variations in the amount and range of drama provision in primary and secondary schools, but the standard of teaching and of pupils' attainment is usually good.

Drama in the early years and primary schools

Well before statutory school age children show an affinity for drama in their play. There is a strong tradition in early years education for including primitive materials, such as sand, water and clay, clothes for 'dressing-up' play, and play in simulated 'home corners'. The roots of drama are all too obvious in children's play in these areas. Pupils in the early years and reception classes frequently act out stories. A play area readily becomes a shop, café, spaceship, travel agency, doctor's surgery or kitchen. The skilled teacher knows how to stimulate and use pupils' play to develop their language, to reinforce number and other skills, to promote co-operation through suggestions and comments and to set up increasingly challenging situations for them to explore: for example, the deliberate selection of the play items provided, and creating two play areas so that the pupils begin to develop plot and narrative as they move between the locations.

From the beginning, there are assemblies which include simple presentations of pupils' work, acting out of stories and action songs, and celebrations of birthdays and religious festivals, especially Christmas and events associated with a range of faiths. Pupils become used to watching performances on television. At this stage, drama is an integral part of the curriculum and rarely identified as a subject in its own right, although sometimes it is carried out in school halls or other designated spaces.

In Year 1, the vast majority of pupils already know the simple rules of listening carefully to instructions, taking turns and staying in role. In a lesson at Overleigh St Mary's Primary School near Chester based on *The Paper Bag Princess* (Munsch 1982), one class was given the ingredients of a story to act out. There was a map, a castle, a frog, a cave, a forest, a prince, and a princess. The teacher, moving in and out of role, led the pupils along a path and on her morning jog the princess discovered a path she had never seen before. The teacher stopped the action to discuss what sort of path it is and later what they might meet and the sounds they might hear. There was some good vocabulary building ('rustling', 'howls') and the class learned to function as a unit. The teacher created a forest of two lines, and the other pupils walked through it. At one point the forest became fairly aggressive but the princess squeezed and scrambled through. There were further pauses for reflection and planning and the class learned much about simple narrative skills and structuring drama.

A Year 2 class at the Martin Wilson Primary School, Shrewsbury, had been studying the theme of water. They had talked about the fate of the *Titanic* and the *Mary Rose* and in an improvisation were asked to imagine diving down to a shipwreck. The information acquired during their work on the theme enabled the pupils to use details which gave the improvisation considerable focus. The teacher constantly referred to specific details: 'What can you see through your diving mask?', 'What is this tube and dial for?' One pupil asked another if he had seen the planks of wood rotting away, 'held together only by a few nails'. The pupils learned much about the properties of water and later wrote about shipwrecks with precision and imagination. At this stage pupils were beginning to take on a role, but, like the Year 1 group, they reacted to suggestions by their teacher en masse. All the children dived together to the bottom of the sea. Their increased maturity and the teacher's emphasis on detail allowed the pupils to contribute their own ideas within the framework provided. This was being deliberately encouraged by the teacher, who remained in role, directing the diving activities for much of the lesson, an effective way of managing the class. For example, pupils could not run around in the hall and become too excited 'because you can't move quickly underwater'.

By the end of Key Stage 1, pupils in these classes have had ample opportunities for dramatic play and have extended such play to dramatic stories. They are familiar with notions of pretence and reality, role play and improvisation, and they have observed and responded to performances by peers and others, adapting their language skills and increasing their vocabulary in response to the demands of different situations. For example, formal presentations have introduced them to the characteristics of standard English. Drama has helped the pupils see the need to work collaboratively and it has played an important part in their learning about a wider range of subjects.

At the Martin Wilson Primary School, slightly older pupils in a mixed Year 3 and 4 class were capable of making a more deliberate attempt at characterisation in a history lesson. Their teacher had spent some time developing their ability to pick up characters and bring them to life in a variety of contexts through the use of circle games, freeze frame and hot-seating techniques. The pupils had developed good levels of skills, reacting quickly to the dialogue of others and taking on appropriate roles within the set context.

The teacher acting in role led a whole class improvisation based on the current topic, the Ancient Greeks. The pupils were asked to imagine that they were to set sail with a captain (their teacher) in search of a silver serpent, and parallels with the story of Jason and the Golden Fleece were underlined. The pupils as crew members talked to the captain about the skills they had to offer and the hazards they expected on the journey. They presented an offering and a prayer to the gods, showing a serious sense of the drama as they carried out these actions individually. Working in groups they acted out their leave-taking from friends and families. The session ended with a discussion, out of role, of ways in which the story might develop.

Towards the end of Key Stage 2, pupils readily incorporate dramatic conventions in a wide range of work and they have a clearer understanding of drama as a separate art form, alongside poetry, stories, dance, music and the visual arts. As an example of the former a Year 5 class at Overleigh St Mary's Primary School worked on the theme of 'Planet Earth', beginning with brief concentration exercises and then a series of questions to introduce them to the notion of conservation, a new aspect of their topic. In groups, pupils presented frozen pictures of conservation issues. Next, the teacher chaired a meeting of countries at the United Nations, pupils choosing the country they wished to represent and conferring with delegates from the same continent. Stage by stage, the urgency of the situation was emphasised by the teacher, who remained in role. The planet was becoming polluted and some nations had to consider large-scale evacuation. The delegates conferred to list the problems faced by their nations and to suggest possible solutions. The lesson was rounded off by the teacher asking pupils to stand close to or further away from a chair placed in the centre of the room as a way of indicating how concerned they were about the planet. He used thought tracking to get individuals to explain why they felt as they did. There was a final review and evaluation of the session.

The teacher had planned the lesson well and structured it carefully. He had clear objectives related to both drama and pupils' learning about the planet. He provided a sound base on which a demanding sequence of activities was built. The pupils recalled and used specific drama strategies and working as a whole class, in groups and individually, their oral skills were developed. They used movement and gesture effectively. The teacher involved pupils in a discussion of ways in which the work might be improved. Their geographical knowledge was reinforced and enhanced through their debating such issues as water shortage, deforestation and poor medicine in Asia and car pollution and ozone depletion in Europe.

Another Year 5 class, this time at Pipworth Junior School in Sheffield, were creating their own version of the Hansel and Gretel story in the school hall; they had prepared partial scripts. The teacher, a gifted storyteller, created for pupils an imaginary setting, and made up rituals and spells to help them enter their roles. Within five minutes pupils had become Hansel or Gretel in the wood. They mimed to extracts from Grieg's incidental music to *Peer Gynt*, concentrating on movement and making effective use of the hall's space. They worked as a whole class to build up a convincing picture of the wicked witch – and the teacher became the witch herself for a few minutes. She then asked them to recall this new person – and pupils learned a great deal about building up a new role without the need for costume or make-up. There was much useful exploration of vocabulary. They moved in role and observed one another,

then met and talked, still in role. There was a brief review of what had been achieved and pupils moved into groups to work on their own plays.

The school lists its aims for drama in the prospectus and the lesson was a good example of 'developing the child's self-confidence and poise and aiding communication with others'. It showed how older pupils can work with scripts and write their own plays, and how drama is able to bring alive the language, ideas and characters of a familiar story.

Clearly, by the end of Key Stage 2 pupils can use the conventions, techniques and vocabulary of drama in designated drama lessons and as a valuable way of learning in other subjects, devise and perform complex plays, and evaluate their own and other people's work. They can create and sustain roles and structure presentations. Work in all three Attainment Targets for English is

Junior House pupils at Roedean, an independent school for girls

thereby enriched; in particular, there have been many opportunities for communication skills to be developed.

Extracurricular drama is popular. At Pipworth Junior School in Sheffield two separate groups meet regularly, about 60 pupils in all, with many more joining in the preparations for ambitious school productions. At a rehearsal the pupils knew their lines, worked well in large groups and had a good grasp of the musical's structure. They knew the plot and had practised their entrances and exits. They used the large space of the school hall well, adjusting their singing and speech to meet the challenge of difficult acoustics and remembered to face an imaginary audience. The cast had acquired impressive skills in movement and dance. The two teachers running the session insisted on high standards of voice, gesture and teamwork and they shaped the emerging performance well, showing pupils how to build scenes to a climax.

Drama in secondary schools

Pupils in secondary schools experience drama in English lessons, though in some schools there will be separate drama lessons or drama within an expressive arts course. In Key Stage 4, drama or theatre studies are popular GCSE subjects. As in primary schools, learning through drama is sometimes a feature of work in other subjects and it continues to be a popular extracurricular activity.

At High Storrs School in Sheffield one very effective English lesson in Year 7 took as its starting point the programmes of study for speaking and listening. Pupils took turns to read an extract from a Betsy Byars novel in different roles, for example as a sports commentator or primary teacher at story time, and as a class compared the differences in tone, expression, pace and general effect. In a well-paced sequence of activities, pupils worked on accent, dialect, standard English, degrees of formality and listening skills. The pupils followed many of the disciplines of good drama, including teamwork, clarity of diction for an audience, sustained concentration, use of specialist terminology and the ability to evaluate their work.

Another Year 7 class, this time at Worden High School, near Preston, began with a text of which they had some knowledge, Lewis Carroll's *Jabberwocky*. The teacher read the poem, using an overhead projector so pupils could see the text and concentrate on the unusual vocabulary. He then asked separate groups to produce moving statues of the creature. They used simple props and worked co-operatively for five minutes. The groups tried out their performances in a continuous sequence. The teacher offered suggestions to the groups on how they might improve their work, such as enlarging and co-ordinating their gestures and speaking more loudly. In a second performance the sequence of improvisations flowed smoothly and pupils' concentration was intense, and voice and gesture were controlled and expressive. A whole performance began to emerge from the groups, who gained enormous satisfaction from the lesson. The teacher called the pupils together and asked them how the improvisations had improved in the second performance. They were keen to explain and they listened carefully to each other's ideas, and they used terms like freeze-frame and tableaux readily and accurately.

The lesson was part of a coherent and varied programme of work which balanced the exploration of ideas and improvisation with a sense of what it is to perform to an audience. The teacher set a brisk pace but created opportunities for pupils to stop and reflect. He had clear objectives for the learning, which he explained to the pupils, and he helped them to internalise their objectives through action and evaluation. The lesson made an excellent contribution to the pupils' social development. All worked co-operatively in small groups and had a powerful experience of effective collaboration as a whole class. Their cultural development was being promoted as they explored a classic poem and appreciated how drama uses voice, space, movement and gesture to make meaning. As they performed the second time the whole class was caught up in the power of their ability to create a fluent sequence out of the separate parts.

At Theale Green School in Berkshire, in a Year 8 lesson which was part of a unit of

Pupils at Theale Green School learn the language of drama

work entitled 'history revisited', the teacher concentrated on the drama strategy known as 'giving witness'. This involves describing a historical event in the first person, 'as if you had been there'. Groups each selected an event – the Fire of London, the Hillsborough disaster, the dismantling of the Berlin Wall, the plague, and the sinking of the *Titanic* – and each was seen from four different points of view, in some cases drawing on knowledge gained from recent history lessons.

For the resulting presentations, pupils stood on the squares of a giant chess board, lit with overhead spot lights, the beginnings and endings of each presentation marked by lights being faded up or down. The lesson succeeded in its aim of introducing a specific drama technique and it drew on pupils' own experiences ('What makes a good story teller?') to introduce the notion of an oral tradition, which was related to the 'giving witness' technique. Pupils followed clear ground rules for behaving and moving in a drama studio, and they used the studio's lighting and space effectively to create atmosphere. Boys and girls worked well together in the groups and four pupils with learning difficulties participated.

Drama in this school is led by two experienced teachers. A departmental handbook comprises a rationale, equal opportunities policy, teaching strategies, extracurricular activities, schemes of work and assessment criteria for Key Stage 3. Assessment and recording are systematic and thorough and relate to particular skills – observing, listening, problem-solving and so on. Another strength of the department's planning is the way a repertoire of drama strategies and associated concepts is introduced progressively during Key Stage 3.

There is a clear sense of pupils' learning the 'language' of the medium. Pupils are fortunate in being able to work in a good, well-equipped studio with outstanding displays which include photographic records of previous productions, key terms and concepts and quotations from theatre practitioners.

St Gregory's RC High School in Warrington timetables drama in an expressive arts programme in Key Stage 3, and there are 70-minute lessons for half the year and 140-minute lessons for the rest. For each year the scheme of work lists skills and ways of organising units of work. Progression is an important part of the planning. For example, 'in Year 9 pupils should begin to look at drama from a more theatrical viewpoint. All the skills of problem-solving etc required in Years 7 and 8 should be built upon, but each piece of work should be regarded as potential performance, possibly for a wider audience.'

A Year 9 class in this school worked on a historical theme, the suffragettes, having read for homework a handout of basic historical background material. The teacher, moving in and out of role, led the pupils to reflect on the main issues and to enact brief scenes to illustrate the attitudes men and women might have held at the turn of the century. Pupils in mixed pairs explored a family conflict about gender roles. Some pairs performed their scenes and, still in role, they revealed their thoughts. In single sex groups of four they acted out a scene which explored possible responses to a woman leaving home. Lastly, as a class the pupils enacted a crowd scene at the Derby in mixed groups, including freeze frames to show relationships and conflicts.

The lesson tackled some complex gender issues. For example, some sequences showed the difficulties men suffered because they were expected to control their feelings. There was time in the lesson for reflection. The teacher sampled pupils' work skilfully, choosing a few improvisations to focus on. She picked up issues about performance skills at appropriate points, for example the direction and structure of improvisation and the need for pupils to project their voices. Some groups produced work of a very high standard. For example, one group of girls improvised a short scene where a group of women washing clothes discussed why one of their friends had left home. Their movements and the dialogue flowed together; they made use of slightly stylised, rhythmic movements so that they created a unified but varied and rather lyrical piece.

A good feature of planning for drama at Bridgewater County High School in Warrington is that in each year, pupils study some history of the theatre: Greeks in Year 7, medieval in Year 8, and Elizabethan in Year 9 as pupils begin to study a Shakespeare play. Within the key stage, pupils are expected to experience, understand and use 25 drama conventions, including mime, ritual, use of video clips and forum theatre, as well as those mentioned elsewhere in this chapter. One Year 9 lesson explored a theme through working on a story read to them by the teacher. The story tells of a young boy who is lonely and made to feel an outsider by his classmates. Locked out of his house and soaked to the skin, he gets invited to a classmate's birthday party by her mother, but he is rejected and made to feel small and inadequate by the other children. Initially, the teacher led a discussion of the story, collecting pupils' ideas on a whiteboard. The lesson moved on to pupils presenting still

Year 8 pupils at Bridgewater County High School explore the Mystery Plays in their lessons on theatre history

images and doing brief thought-tracking to explore the issues identified by the class.

The teacher worked in and out of role, interviewing individuals who took on roles from the story and explaining their actions and feelings. She skilfully questioned the pupil who was acting as the central character and elicited comments about other characters' behaviour as a result. Moral issues were handled with tact and pupils made many sensitive points which showed a good understanding of the story. This understanding was converted into dramatic form: the pupils' exploration of character, motivation and behaviour were considerable in a short period of time.

By the end of the key stage, pupils in many schools have acquired a wide range of skills and can use them effectively in bringing a text to life, creating characters, exploring a theme or developing abilities listed in the NC Order for English (DFE 1995), such as adapting talk to suit the circumstances

(AT1), reflecting on the motivation and behaviour of characters (AT2), and developing their use of dialogue to convey character (AT3). Pupils will have been introduced to Shakespeare, usually in Year 9, and will have some familiarity with different styles and traditions of drama. They will be able to appreciate good drama, whether presented in the classroom by their peers, in the theatre, or on television, and discuss it using appropriate terminology and selecting examples to make a point. In schools where there are good links between the arts, some pupils will have experienced music drama or dance drama.

Moving into Key Stage 4, pupils' experience of drama varies considerably. Within English, the programmes of study specify the kinds of play that ought to be read, list scripts and dialogue as key skills in writing and emphasise that pupils should be given opportunities to participate in a wide range of drama activities and study the

GCSE pupils at Newfield School perform street theatre in Sheffield city centre

language used in drama and role-play.

In a Year 11 examination class at Newfield School in Sheffield, pupils drew on their considerable knowledge of drama concepts and disciplines. They ran through a series of voice warm-up exercises – chants and rhythms to develop voice and fluency – and then moved into a sequence of improvisations based on a situation in a *Relate* office. Pupils had prepared carefully for the lesson and worked well in groups, which changed as family representatives visited the offices. The pupils created convincing fictions, building and sustaining roles and situations; introducing and resolving conflict; adapting language to meet the needs of the interviews; controlling voice, expression, gesture and movement; and showing good social awareness and background knowledge. Pupils took on responsibility for negotiating roles and for structuring their presentations. They explored a number of sensitive issues, including family conflicts, sexuality and stereotyping within the conventions of drama.

The teacher led the initial exercises, provided good training in concentration and delivery and intervened occasionally to encourage a deeper response to complex issues. For much of the lesson she observed the groups in action, noting pupils' achievements, taking photographs which would form part of the evidence for assessment and occasionally modelling effective techniques. Standards of presentation here benefited from having available a drama studio with blackout, simple lighting and a few props.

In this school an experienced drama teacher leads a small team in providing a separate drama course in Year 8. In other years drama features in mainstream English. This is an unusual model but ensures that expertise is used effectively. As is often the case, given the presence on the staff of an enthusiast, extracurricular drama activities flourish, with two major productions a year – in recent times these have included *A Midsummer Night's Dream (*Shakespeare), *Our Day Out* (Willy Russell), *Adrian Mole*

(Sue Townsend) and *Les Miserables* (the play not the musical). The school participates in the city's children's drama festival and the drama club specialises in experimental theatre, typically involving the audience in its shows.

Drama in Key Stage 4 often spills out of the classroom into other aspects of school life. At West Derby Comprehensive School for Boys in Liverpool a Year 11 GCSE group worked during lunchtime on a presentation of Jim Cartwright's play *Two*. This explores the relationship between a married couple in a pub: a bullying, aggressive man systematically humiliating his wife. The two boys involved in the extract were word perfect and had the confidence and control to use pauses, lack of eye contact, silences and body language to create convincing characters. They understood the tense relationship between the couple and changed the tempo and pace to suggest menace and recoil. The boy playing the female character was not at all self-conscious.

The group explained that they enjoyed working together in a climate of trust. They have developed personal confidence which helps them in other areas of their school life. Their teacher has given the boys opportunities to visit the theatre, join workshops and work with members of her evening class. Many are considering taking A-level theatre studies.

In the same school, a Year 10 group only five months into their GCSE course prepared and performed a 25-minute piece on the theme of 'Changing Attitudes to Violence'. This was presented at the LEA's conference with the same title, a high-profile event with a national speaker, workshops and two other drama presentations from primary schools, held at the conference centre of Liverpool

Football Club. The 15 boys in the group used workshop techniques to explore the idea of a famous footballer ending up alone in a bedsit at the age of 40. Through a series of flashbacks, they presented three key points in his life: his wedding day, when he drinks too much and spends time with the lads instead of his wife; the birth of his first child – he wasn't there; and the final splitting with his wife after striking her. The group then re-ran each event, asking if things could have been different and showing realistic alternative resolutions. The boys worked as an ensemble, all on stage throughout, and each taking on a variety of roles, with the narrative maintained by the boy playing the footballer. The presentation was remarkable for its seamless integration of drama skills and conventions, including flashback, repetition, still image, mime and thought-tracking. Conference delegates received the performance enthusiastically.

These examples illustrate how good examination syllabuses, the motivation and enthusiasm of pupils and the skills of an experienced teacher can combine to provide experience of drama of a high standard. At its best, the work shows pupils learning and putting into practice a wide range of skills and techniques; experimenting successfully with different forms of presentation; showing a high degree of teamwork; using resources well; exploring issues and characters in depth; and adopting an open and critical approach to their own work and that of others.

Beyond Key Stage 4, A-level theatre studies courses are popular and often stimulate work of a very high standard. There were lessons in which pupils prepared for their final assessment, working on themes chosen by themselves. At High Storrs School

A-level theatre studies pupils at High Storrs School

in Sheffield these were often complex and emotive: the workings of fate, the impact of a child's death on a family, or an unexpected pregnancy, for example. Pupils used their knowledge of theatre and their varied experience of drama work to produce highly disciplined performances, often using non-naturalistic styles, shaping ideas well, portraying emotions, setting up tension for specific effect and building in subtle changes of pace. Such work was characterised by careful structuring and excellent voice control. One piece combined effective formal and informal dialogue, verse, choral delivery and sounds. There was an appreciation of both the theoretical underpinning of the work and the values inherent in the presentation. Even at a late stage in the course, pupils had the confidence to make adjustments in the light of their own reflection and evaluations. Many pupils had become proficient in their handling of

staging, lighting, sound and other technical aspects of production. The very best A-level teaching and learning combine background information, theatrical techniques and close textual study, all bound together in a very practical sequence of work.

Finally, as part of their theatre studies course, girls at Roedean, an independent school, took part in a workshop on the use of masks, led by a member of a professional theatre group. Pupils had previously made their own masks out of paper bags: the front showed how they would like to be seen, and the back showed how they thought they were normally seen. The pupils learned quickly about dominant characteristics and, wearing professionally made masks, they explored simple but effective techniques which relied on silence and limited movement. Pupils came to understand the power of the mask – how it is possible to hide behind one and live through it.

In conclusion

This chapter draws on observations from the inspection of drama in a large number of schools, including primary schools in disadvantaged areas and favoured schools in the independent sector. It highlights examples of good drama as children move through the school system and illustrates how progression in drama can be achieved. It recognises that good drama in schools draws on a rich field of reference and that any of the lessons described here might be placed on a spectrum running from drama as performance to participation in drama to gain greater control of language, enlarge vocabulary and explore relationships and emotions. Teachers have clear aims and objectives for their lessons or units of work: to improve pupils' knowledge of accent; to teach the use of specific techniques; to explore a theme; to allow children to experience what it is like to take on another role; to get to know how Macbeth might be staged; or to prepare a full-scale production. Teachers then select the approach that is most likely to help them achieve those objectives, all the time seeking to build on pupils' previous experiences and achievements. Schemes of work and drama handbooks help to map out a school's approach to drama. A structure which many schools have found helpful is the distinction which may be made between creating and performing in drama and appreciating and appraising it.

The focus of this chapter, and of the book, is good practice in the arts, but wide-ranging inspection shows that there are too many schools where drama does not flourish:

- no drama seen during a week-long inspection, because drama is somehow seen as an unnecessary luxury or a risky activity
- staff lack the expertise to teach drama or use drama as an approach across the curriculum
- drama is restricted to annual plays performed for parents

and so on. Conversely, there are schools where drama is well established but the other arts subjects are poorly represented.

What can schools do to maintain or improve their work in drama?

- Define pupils' drama curriculum in terms of experiences (in and out of the classroom), attainment and methods of teaching and learning, and formulate schemes of work to outline drama practice and support everyday, routine planning.

- Ensure that there is good leadership in teaching drama but that provision and good standards are not reliant on a single and dedicated enthusiast.

- Plan for a steady improvement in facilities. Resources for drama vary unduly in degree and appropriateness. Within this relatively small sample, schools used a cramped conventional classroom, school hall, drama studio, near-derelict hut, home-made staging in a classroom and school theatre rivalling that used by many professional companies.

- Have a system for assessing pupils' progress and attainment in drama, relating standards achieved to a clearly articulated scheme of work.

- In secondary schools, protect the place of drama in the curriculum, especially in Key Stage 4, where there is increasing pressure from vocational options.

- Consider sources of further development outside the school: courses for staff, local theatres, higher education institutions, LEAs, theatre-in-education groups.

- Make explicit drama's contribution to pupils' personal, social, moral and spiritual development, and take care in exploring complex themes or 'issues' to ensure that their treatment is not superficial.

Notes

[1] A problem-solving game in which pupils take on the role of a group presented with a certain number of 'givens' and a decision to make.

[2] A point within the drama which is held still as though it were a photograph or stopped video image.

[3] Similar to freeze-frame but pupils are asked to work together to present a 'statue' or still image which represents the essential nature of a situation, relationship or incident.

[4] The action of the drama is halted and a character is asked to express what he or she is feeling or thinking.

[5] A type of simulation in which a small group acts out a situation and is observed by the rest of the class in order to explore a number of issues. The action can be stopped at any point, decisions challenged and the course of action changed.

[6] A character responds in role to a sequence of questions from the group.

5 Music

Janet Mills HMI

SPECIALIST ADVISER FOR MUSIC

Music in the curriculum

Music is an important part of the nursery, primary and secondary curriculum. The *desirable outcomes for learning* (SCAA 1996a) by pupils in nursery settings include:

- exploring sound

- responding in a variety of ways to what they hear

- using musical instruments to express their ideas and communicate their feelings

- through music, showing an increasing ability to use their imagination, listen, and observe.

From the ages of 5 to 14 pupils follow a National Curriculum in music (DFE 1995) that is based on the activities of performing, composing, listening and appraising. Teachers are encouraged to bring together requirements from both *performing and composing* and *listening and appraising* wherever possible.

Once pupils have completed the National Curriculum, the courses that schools offer can lead to qualifications, including GCSE, GCSE (short course), GCE (A and AS), BTEC National and GNVQ Part 2, in subjects such as music, music technology, performing arts or expressive arts.

Clearly, schools can, if they wish, extend their provision beyond the minimum required by the *desirable outcomes for learning*, the National Curriculum or public examinations. The great majority do so, and offer extra instrumental lessons or the opportunity to participate in ensembles such as choirs, rock groups or bands to some or all of their pupils.

Inspection findings in music

The findings of national inspection (OFSTED 1993, 1995, 1996a, 1996b; Mills 1997a, 1997b) show that there is much to celebrate about music in schools. For several years, music has been the best taught subject in primary schools. The quality of teaching in Key Stage 3 is improving, and it is already very high from Key Stage 4 onwards. The early signs from the inspection of nursery settings are encouraging. Most institutions successfully promote pupils' awareness of sound, and develop their observational skills, although some other *desirable learning outcomes* are less evident.

It would, though, be wrong to suggest that all is well with music in schools, that Key Stages 1, 2 and 4 and post-16 can all look after themselves, that Key Stage 3 will right itself in a few years, or that all the nursery curriculum needs is more time to establish itself. However good the music in a school, teachers are continually looking for ways of making it even better. Moreover, these inspection findings are averages, and for every lesson or school that is above average roughly one falls below.

Inspectors have found that there are some specific and persistent problems that affect the quality of the music provision to some degree in more than a few schools. They can occur at any stage of pupils' education, but tend to cluster in particular key stages. They include difficulties with:

- *Continuity and progression.* Lack of continuity in pupils' experience of music means that they do not consolidate their knowledge, understanding and skills. Lack of progression means that the teaching fails to promulgate the content of the subject – skills, knowledge and understanding – incrementally. Thus pupils do much the same things, say, in Year 3 as in Year 2. Continuity and progression are issues in Key Stage 2, when pupils may have more than one music teacher at a time, and their teachers may not exchange information about their progress. Pupils may have one teacher for their class music lessons, a second for a singing lesson for the whole year group, and a third for some optional recorder lessons at lunchtime. At the end of the year, pupils may transfer to another teacher for their class music lessons, and this teacher may know very little about their previous work. Difficulties with continuity and progression may increase when pupils move to a new school for, or during, Key Stage 3. Secondary teachers who are uncertain about the curriculum that pupils followed in their previous school often underestimate their prior learning, and so secondary pupils' progress is weak. Singing is a frequent casualty at this stage.

- *Exploiting pupils' musical creativity and developing their musical imagination.* The curriculum that pupils follow up to the end of Key Stage 1 often focuses unduly on simple mechanical exercises that teach skills outside a musical context. Pupils have insufficient opportunity to engage in the performing, composing, listening and appraising activities that can move them towards the *desirable outcomes for learning*, and which the National Curriculum require. There is a related problem on some courses at post-16, when pupils may effectively have a two-year curricular break from the broad practical activities that were the main focus of their work in Key Stage 4, and are likely to become the focus again if they continue music in higher education. Music teaching at post-16 often focuses unduly on the requirements of specific examination papers from a very early stage of the course, and can resemble the musically sterile activities found at Key Stage 1, only adapted for pupils who are considerably older and more experienced.

- *Participation in music at school.* A large majority of pupils choose not to study music in Key Stage 4. The very low take-up for music at post-16 follows from the high level of drop-out at the end of Year 9.

This chapter focuses on some schools that have made progress with at least one of these issues. It consists of linked examples of lessons or management strategies that were successful in their context. The examples of lessons have been organised in an order that is roughly chronological, as this may illuminate some of the possibilities for continuity and progression in music education for pupils aged 3–18. They are grouped loosely into sections that focus on:

- Nursery and Key Stages 1 and 2
- Key Stage 3
- Key Stage 4 and post-16.

Music in nurseries and Key Stages 1 and 2

ISSUES: exploiting pupils' musical creativity and developing their musical imagination in the nursery and during Key Stage 1; continuity and progression during Key Stage 2.

Mention continuity and progression in a primary school and the conversation often turns to the staffing of music lessons. Some people believe that the key to continuity and progression in primary schools is teaching by 'specialists'. Others believe equally passionately that music should be taught by class teachers. Rigorous discussion of this matter would require careful definition of the term 'music specialist'. Is a music specialist anyone who teaches a class other than their own for music, or should they also have some special expertise in music? If so, should this

be reflected in qualifications? If so, at what level? Should the range of their qualifications or expertise cover the full range of the National Curriculum, including composing, or is expertise in performing on two or three instruments sufficient? Should they have taken music as a main subject during their initial teacher training? Should they have trained for the primary phase? Do they need Qualified Teacher Status at all?

No doubt, discussion of these questions will continue. The findings of inspection, meanwhile, point to schools with good music provision where all or some of the lessons are taught by various categories of music specialists, and others where all the music lessons are taught by class teachers. They also point to schools with and without specialists where the music provision is of poor quality. We do not know of a single way of deploying teachers or organising a music curriculum that works wherever it is applied. Headteachers try to find ways of providing music that work in their school, taking account of the strengths of their teachers and the resources, including finance, that are available.

Some headteachers have attempted to improve continuity and progression by deploying just one teacher for music throughout the school. This arrangement is common in middle schools, and quite frequent in very small primary schools, where it may be feasible for one of the class teachers to teach each class for music, and still spend most of the week with his or her class. At its best, this arrangement works well. The sole music teacher may be a gifted teacher whose curriculum covers the full range of the National Curriculum, and makes appropriate and progressively greater demands of all pupils as they get older. The music teacher is allowed sufficient time to work thoroughly and frequently with each class. He or she builds up a musical knowledge of all the pupils in the school and, if also a class teacher, makes valuable links between pupils' attainment in music, and that in other subjects. The attainment of all the pupils across the full range of the programmes of study in music is well beyond the expectations for their age.

Other schools have rejected this strategy. In some cases the reason is financial: the school is too large for one class teacher to teach all the classes for music, and does not have the resources to employ a floating music teacher. In other cases, the strategy has been rejected as a matter of principle. The headteacher may take the view that it is not constructive for music to be singled out as a special subject that requires different teachers. He or she may also consider that pupils benefit from having teachers who work with them in several subjects.

For a variety of reasons, the very great majority of primary schools have more than one music teacher, and so communication between teachers is necessary, and the issue of planning for continuity and progression has to be addressed overtly. So, in most schools, must the issue of raising some teachers' confidence to teach music. Despite national inspection findings that show that music is taught with higher quality than any other subject, many class teachers believe that they teach music less effectively than anything else.

Perhaps because composing is a relatively new area of the music curriculum for many teachers, schools that are trying to raise teachers' confidence and improve their music curriculum will often start by focusing on it.

At Pashley Down Infant School, Eastbourne, the headteacher is using composing to encourage all the teachers to contribute to pupils' musical development. For the equivalent of one term of the year, each class's weekly music lesson is taught jointly by the headteacher and the class teacher. The headteacher starts the lesson with activities that require pupils to copy and organise environmental and other sounds. She builds effectively on pupils' individual responses, and systematically develops their use of language, ability to recognise pattern in sound, and ability to observe fine differences in individual sounds. Later in the lesson, it is usual for teachers of Year 2 pupils to withdraw a group of pupils for a related composing activity, and their work is appraised at the end of the lesson by the whole class. In some lessons, the pupils record their composition using symbols that they have devised. Completed compositions are sometimes shared with the whole school in assembly, and this helps teachers to be aware of the headteacher's expectations of pupils in different years at the school.

At Sheringham Primary School, Norfolk, the class teachers have been working with the music co-ordinator on the development of the music curriculum for several years. Pupils' attainment is above the national expectation at the end of Key Stage 1 and at the end of Key Stage 2. Pupils are encouraged to use their imagination in music lessons from their first days at school. They also learn the skills that they need to express their musical ideas. For example, pupils in the nursery follow the teacher's signals for loud/quiet when singing, and when accompanying their singing using percussion instruments. Pupils in reception also

A nursery pupil at Sheringham Primary School paints in response to 'Spring' from Vivaldi's *Four Seasons*

recognise, apply and talk about *opposites*, including fast/slow. The photograph shows a nursery pupil painting in response to 'Spring' from Vivaldi's *Four Seasons*. Her teacher wrote:

'We worked on a one-to-one basis, first discussing the frieze which we had made as a group for the nursery walls which included lambs, ducklings, blossom and spring flowers. I asked the children, while listening to the music, to imagine the lambs jumping and the blossoms bursting on the trees. I asked them to try to put the sounds which they were hearing on to their painting … The children were very enthusiastic, liked using the

A pupil at Sheringham School conducts a pictorial score

headphones and were eager to express themselves.

To encourage some of the less expressive children I drew brush strokes on the backs of their hands and used my fingers to tap the rhythms on the paper, sometimes humming the melody.

The results were surprising. The children did not try to draw a picture but painted spirals, zig-zags and short and long lines with dots all over the paper, sometimes over existing paint. They painted until the end of the concerto and then stopped, immediately putting down their brushes ... Many came back, asking for more.'

Midway through Year 1, a class had worked in four groups to compose music that accompanied part of a story they had made up about a princess and a dragon. The pupils did not simply copy natural sounds with their instruments, and add them to a story to provide sound effects. Each group of pupils used a range of percussion instruments to play short remembered musical structures that conveyed the mood of their part of the story: peaceful, playful, noisy or angry.

Some of the pupils' compositions are performed by a full class. The second photograph on page 63 shows a pupil conducting a pictorial score of a composition inspired by mini-beasts.

The music co-ordinator at Sherard Primary School, near Melton Mowbray, is a full-time class teacher. For several years she has provided training for her colleagues. They use the school's scheme of work to provide a rich and varied music curriculum that emphasises composing. The teachers approach music with an unusual and welcome degree of confidence.

At Brookside Primary School, near Stockport, staff development and curriculum development are addressed together, and the headteacher leads by example in encouraging teachers to take more risks in their music teaching, and to observe and build on the pupils' views about how their compositions are progressing. At Brookside, 'safe' pentatonic work is heard rarely: pupils are encouraged to choose the resources, including notes and rhythms, that they need for their compositions. The headteacher often organises her music lessons so that she does not need to draw on her own skills as a performer, thus showing a class teacher with a less extensive musical background that he or she could achieve similar results from the class. Groups of pupils who are working on compositions that make experimental use of notes and rhythms are sometimes allowed to develop their work in public areas of the school such as the hall or corridors: work-in-progress that might have sounded to a casual eavesdropper like unthinking fiddling with instruments can be seen by passing teachers

A group of composers at Brookside Primary School develop their work by 'thinking aloud'

and pupils to be the *thinking-aloud* in which pupils who are devising a joint composition must engage.

In some schools, examples of teaching by class teachers can be used by co-ordinators to inspire other class teachers. The following lesson was taught to a Year 5 class by a teacher who was in her second year of teaching, and had no qualifications in music.

Two pupils who had recently started cello lessons had brought their instruments to the lesson. The teacher organised them to provide a demonstration of *high, low, higher* and *lower* on cellos. Next, there was demonstration and discussion of *steps* and *leaps* on cellos. This led to a composing activity. In pairs, the pupils composed question and answer phrases, thinking about their use of *steps, leaps, high, low, higher* and *lower*. The teacher circulated round the pairs, helping them to develop their ideas. The lesson ended with detailed appraisal, discussion and development of two compositions in front of the class.

During this lesson, the pupils appeared to grow musically in front of your eyes. They already had reasonable skills in playing tuned percussion with two mallets, and they understood that *high* and *low* are relative terms, that what is *high* for a cello might be *low* for a violin. The teacher elicited demonstrations from pupils, and used them constructively when instructing the whole class. She encouraged pupils to lengthen their *questions*. She developed their verbal analysis of their peers' compositions. She expected pupils to remember their compositions, and repeat them so that others could analyse what they were doing.

There were no short cuts, such as 'safe' use of pentatonic scales, or giving some pupils untuned instruments. The teacher's expectations were very high, and proved to be realistic.

Meadow Vale Primary School, Bracknell, has a long history of teaching composing, and enabling the music co-ordinator to monitor and support the work of her colleagues by participating in some of their lessons. The music co-ordinator felt in need of another view on composing at the school, and secured this by working with a professional composer over several months. The school showed the value they placed on this project by the way that they deployed their staff. Class teachers always taught jointly with the composer, and the music co-ordinator was released from teaching her class so that she could be present. Some composing of a very high standard resulted.

A class of pupils in Year 5 and Year 6 were attending their second lesson with the composer. The pupils in Year 6 worked in separate groups from those in Year 5: they have had more experience of composing than the younger pupils, so are expected to show higher attainment, and need different teaching. A total of six groups of pupils were continuing work on compositions intended to have a *mysterious* or *sleepy* mood. The lesson started with detailed appraisal led by the composer of two *mysterious* compositions, and ended with detailed appraisal of two *sleepy* compositions. The composer struck a balance between eliciting and developing the pupils' ideas, and introducing her own.

For the rest of the lesson the teacher and composer worked with each of the groups in turn, spending a total of about five minutes with each one. Some of the groups used notation of various sorts as an *aide memoire*.

The compositions that were developing had some very interesting features. In one group, pupils were securely repeating *4 against 3* rhythms. Some groups experimented with ways of introducing contrast by making subtle, minimal, changes in *ostinati*. Several groups tried to use repetition, and deviation from repetition, in ways that would surprise, but not shock, an audience. Although the compositions were not complete they were securely formed: when asked by the composer, the pupils could take their compositions to pieces and perform the individual parts, change the parts in accordance with the composer's suggestions, and then reassemble the piece by playing all the revised parts together. Some of the pupils' suggestions showed that they were learning to dissect and reassemble compositions with their ears and eyes, and talk about what they could hear and see: they would comment on the way that an individual was playing, and then suggest an often subtle change that they believed would improve the overall effect of the piece. There was a difference in the quality of the work produced by the two year groups: a *mysterious* composition devised by pupils in Year 6 conveyed suspense more effectively, because the pupils managed to build up the intensity of their playing very gradually, and timed the changes between sections of their piece very skilfully.

In 1994 Timothy Hackworth Primary School, Shildon, listed the introduction of composing as a priority in the school development plan, and the teachers agreed that they needed to obtain some outside help. Since then, a consultant has been employed to work with each class for two 6-week blocks each year. He team-teaches with each class teacher, who follows up the work in between their joint lessons. The attainment of the pupils in composing is often very high, and the effects of this are starting to have an impact on the pupils' work in the other activities of the music National Curriculum. The impact of pupils' composing on their listening and appraising was shown in the following lesson.

This was the Year 2 pupils' weekly listening and appraising lesson with their class teacher. First, they talked about what they could remember of the piece of music listened to during the previous week: some Gregorian chant. Next, they listened to the piece chosen for this week, Elton John's arrangement of the Beatles' song *Lucy in the Sky with Diamonds*. The teacher stopped the recording at planned moments to ask the pupils to predict what might happen next. She encouraged the pupils to talk about what they could hear, and relate the Elton John arrangement to their own compositions. Finally, she played the entire song again, to give pupils an opportunity to relate the points made in discussion to the music.

The pupils learnt to see the patterns in the structure of the Elton John arrangement, for example the way that slow and fast sections alternate, and used vocabulary including *tempo, dynamics, mood* and *texture* appropriately when talking about the changes in mood that occurred with the changes in tempo. They talked about some ways in which they could try to create similar effects in their compositions.

At Fountaindale Special School, near Mansfield, for pupils with physical disabilities, composing is firmly established in the music curriculum. The pupils enjoy composing on their own, or with a teacher, and the teachers also encourage them to contribute ideas to group compositions.

Eleven pupils in Years 4–6 were working on a composition linked to a topic on native Australians. They were trying to describe sunrise, and its transition to morning. Initially, the pupils worked individually or with an adult: they used a keyboard or a xylophone, and were reminded by the teacher-in-charge to think about which of their sounds should be long/short, high/low or loud/quiet. The adults encouraged pupils to develop and lengthen their musical ideas, and to think about appropriate ways of writing down their work. Once the pupils had some secure individual ideas they were expected to collaborate with another pupil, and then work in a group of five or six pupils. Finally, the teacher-in-charge told a story which provided a structure enabling these two compositions to be combined.

One striking feature of this lesson was the stillness of the pupils when a teacher asked them to prepare themselves for the final performance of their composition. In addition, the pupils' physical control of the instruments improved as they relaxed into the lesson, and became absorbed by their work.

The musical life of Kates Hill Primary School, Dudley, is unusually varied. As well as attending regular class music lessons, pupils may learn instruments, including steel pans, keyboard and recorder, and Asian dance. The teachers try to take account of the varied musical experiences of pupils in their class music lessons.

The music curriculum at Kates Hill was developed over several years, and is documented in detail. This is a factor in the high and ever-increasing expectations of pupils as they move through Key Stage 1 and Key Stage 2, and ensures that pupils learn the skills they need to attain appropriately in composing, performing, listening and appraising. There is a strong emphasis on learning to internalise music, i.e. to hear music in one's head.

A class of Year 6 pupils were drawing graphic scores: their compositions had to include a drone and use variations in dynamics and pitch. At first sight it appeared that this was an amusical

A steel pans performance for parents at Kates Hill Primary school

exercise: the pupils were drawing without using instruments and without making musical sounds. However, conversation with the pupils revealed that they knew exactly which instruments would play each line of their composition, and were experimenting with the various sorts of sounds that the instruments could produce in their minds, selecting the sounds they wanted, and then notating them. Some pupils had decided who would be playing particular instruments, and were writing parts that were thought to lie within their technical reach. As the lesson developed, some pupils collected instruments and started to try out compositions. Occasionally, parts of a score were found to be not what the composer had wanted, or quiet, thoughtful contact with instruments generated new ideas that the composer preferred. The scores were adjusted and became accurate records of the finished compositions.

Most of these case studies have described developments that have occurred over several years. However, considerable change can sometimes be effected in only two or three years. At Longmead Primary School, Hillingdon, a music co-ordinator has developed a scheme of work which allows teachers to bring together requirements concerning performing and composing, and listening and appraising, wherever possible. As individual teachers have started to implement this scheme of work, the attainment of the pupils has started to rise. The standard of composition in Key Stage 2, in particular Year 6, is already a strength of the school. The pupils are taught to listen to and analyse music from a range of times and cultures, and their compositions explore some of the structures and styles that they have found during this work.

Music in Key Stage 3

ISSUE: continuity and progression

Starting at secondary school often brings pupils important new musical experiences, including the opportunity to work with new resources, in special music accommodation, and with some new musicians, both pupils and teachers. However, where the transition between the primary and the secondary music curriculum is not managed well, a move to a new school carries a risk that pupils will cease to achieve as highly as they did at primary school, and not make adequate progress during Key Stage 3.

Some indications of the standards which pupils in Year 7 and Year 8 are capable, given a smooth transition from Key Stage 2 to Key Stage 3, are exemplified at Corbridge Middle School, Northumberland. The music curriculum at Corbridge is broad and emphasises composition, which is taught systematically from Year 5. The music that the pupils listen to and appraise includes that of some contemporary composers, including Peter Maxwell Davies, and they are encouraged to take themselves seriously as composers. The pupils are well-versed in jazz. They are all taught to play recorder, keyboard and tuned percussion, and to develop good working techniques on all of these instruments. They also sing well. The school's scheme of work includes some activities drawn from a published scheme, and they are typically used with pupils who are one or two years younger than those for whom they were intended.

Longfield Middle School, Harrow, has a music curriculum with a different flavour, but provides an equally compelling insight into the capabilities of pupils in Year 7. A curriculum which has grown from activities in a published scheme is used as a vehicle for stimulating the enthusiasm and intellectual curiosity of pupils. Published backing tracks are used to bring to the classroom instruments that the school does not possess, but are set aside as soon as they start to limit the pupils' work, perhaps because the pupils want to experiment with varying the tempo of a performance. The pupils learn to sing in a range of styles. During the inspection visit they sang *Blue Suede Shoes* with uncanny authenticity, improvised percussion accompaniments appropriate to the song, and talked with authority and used musical terms to describe the differences between some recorded examples of rock 'n' roll and skiffle.

Coseley School, near Wolverhampton, uses curriculum materials devised by primary and secondary teachers and advisers in Dudley LEA to smooth the transfer between primary and secondary school, and increase the chance that pupils' attainment in music will forge ahead once they arrive at secondary school. Called 'Moving On', the materials are based around four songs about transport that the pupils learn at primary school, using lively backing tracks if their teachers wish, and also sing during an induction visit to Coseley shortly before the end of Year 6. There are also some optional composing activities and listening exercises, based on compositions by pupils in Key Stage 4, that can be completed in Year 6.

The teacher's certainty that Year 7 pupils have four songs in common, and his experience that virtually all pupils enjoy the songs, frees him to plan a first Year 7 lesson that uses them as a springboard for challenging composing, performing, listening and appraising activities. The self-consciousness that often arises when Year 7 pupils are asked to start singing at secondary school by learning a new song in new surroundings and seated among pupils that they do not know is avoided. The routines of the music department at Coseley are introduced in a practical context.

A Year 7 class's second lesson began with an aural exercise based on the four songs. Three pupils who had volunteered to spend some time during a lunchbreak practising in the music room took it in turns to play a total of a dozen melodic fragments from the songs. The other pupils had to identify which song a fragment came from, state the words, and explain the position of the fragment in the song.

Next, the pupils worked on all the songs, responding to advice from the teacher about how to improve the quality of their singing. As this section of the lesson developed, the pupils also answered questions about the music and their singing that required them to develop their ability to replay and rewind music in their heads, increase the focus with which they listened to and evaluated their own singing, and think ever harder.

Finally, the pupils divided into groups to start an activity that would occupy them for several further lessons: composition of an instrumental link between a given pair of songs, based on melodic fragments from both of them.

Many other schools try to establish and sustain momentum throughout Key Stage 3 without the use of bridging materials. In some cases the curriculum is based on musical tasks that appear quite simple in principle, and which pupils carry out to a very high standard of technical accuracy and musical expression.

One of the projects completed by Year 7 pupils at Highfields School, Wolverhampton, is based on the theme of 'Water', and develops and consolidates pupils' use of the graphic notation that most encountered in their primary schools. Early in the project, pupils use the worksheet illustrated opposite while they listen to recordings of pieces for three players. First, they have to work out, by noticing when each of the three parts enters and ceases, which of the four scores on the right-hand side of the worksheet matches the piece. Second, they have to spot which one of the 12 *ostinati* on the left-hand side of the worksheet each player is repeating.

Later in the project, pupils use the same principles to compose their own *Water Music*, and notate it. They use tuned percussion instruments, and are expected to show control of texture, tempo, dynamics and pitch. They listen to some other music that portrays characteristics of water, including the storm from Beethoven's Pastoral Symphony, Smetana's *Vltava*, and Chopin's 15th Prelude (*Raindrop*). The photograph shows some Year 7 pupils at work on their composition. It also shows another feature of the work at Highfields: the use of display to reinforce pupils' knowledge of the names and properties of instruments, and to present them with role models of musicians. The picture of a French horn player is not a commercial poster, but a high-quality photograph of a Highfields pupil who plays French horn.

Work in Year 8 at Highfields includes bluesy/jazzy improvisation based on a version of *Good King Wenceslas*. A project in Year 9

Year 7 pupils at Highfields School composing *Water Music*

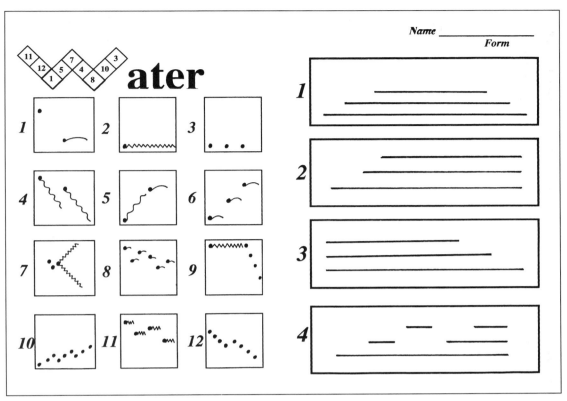

A *Water* worksheet from Highfields School

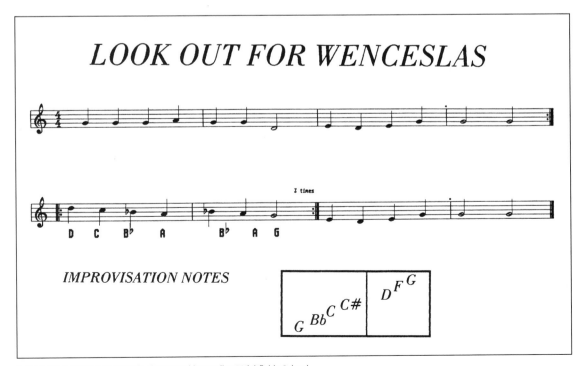

A *Look Out for Wenceslas* music sheet used by pupils at Highfields School

A *Twinkle Twinkle Little Mars* music sheet used by pupils at Highfields School

is based on a 5/4 version of *Twinkle, Twinkle Little Star*. Examples of worksheets for both of these projects are illustrated.

Music at Springwell School, Staveley, is taught by two job sharers. Their scheme of work for Key Stage 3 is documented in detail, to try to ensure that classes who are taught by different teachers have similar experiences. The lessons often include a sequence of short varied tasks that focus the pupils' concentration and prepare them physically and mentally for the main challenge of the lesson. Imaginative and skilful ordering of these tasks reduces the predictability of lessons, and leads to

musical performances and compositions of a high standard.

A Year 7 lesson opened with clapping of 2-bar rhythms from notation, and later by ear. Some pupils spotted that the rhythms were drawn from a syncopated modal instrumental piece in two parts that they had rehearsed in the previous lesson, and the rhythm of this piece was reconstructed on the board from memory using the 2-bar cells that had already been clapped. Now that pupils' ears and memories had been prepared, the teacher turned their attention to the rehearsal of the modal piece. The pupils moved to the instruments that they would be playing: mainly keyboards, but also some xylophones, a cornet and a clarinet. A period of whole class teaching was followed by some independent rehearsal, and a secure class performance ensued. The pupils all had workable techniques on their instruments. Next, each part one player was paired with a part two player, and they rehearsed the piece as a duet. Some duets were performed for appraisal by the class. One performance was flawless. The other pupils showed through their comments and their efforts to correct their mistakes that they understood what was required, and were working steadily towards it.

The lesson ended, as it had begun, with the whole class working together. A song was rehearsed. Some of the pupils spotted that some of its rhythms were drawn from the instrumental piece.

Elsewhere, the curriculum seems at first sight to contain activities that are very similar to those in many other schools, but a subtle twist in the way they are implemented leads to some distinctive outcomes.

At St Saviour's and St Olave's School, Southwark, pupils in Year 8 reinforce their knowledge of staff notation by finding some words that can be made using the letters A–G, such as BAG and CABBAGE, and then write them on a stave. This is a task that has been found for many years in many schools, and which has attracted criticism from inspectors because it involves no performing, composing, listening or appraising. However, at St Saviour's and St Olave's all these activities are included in a challenging manner: the pupils take their notated words to a keyboard, play them, and compose a melody using some of them. They play the final versions of their melody to their peers, who try, often with considerable success, to work out by ear which words have been used.

Year 8 composition at St Saviour's and St Olave's School

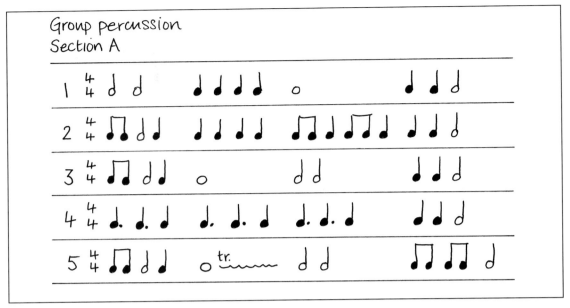

The A section of a Year 8 ternary composition at St Saviour's and St Olave's School

One of the hallmarks of the music curriculum at St Saviour's and St Olave's is the attention paid to consolidating and applying pupils' knowledge of staff notation, without limiting pupils' compositions to music that could sensibly or reasonably be notated on a stave. The illustration shows a score that five Year 8 pupils produced for the A section of a composition in ternary form (ABA). The task required that the B section be improvised and played from memory.

The music curriculum at The Dormston School, Dudley, like that at St Saviour's and St Olave's, includes some well-tried ideas that are developed into challenging activities.

A lesson for pupils in Year 7 ended with an opportunity to watch a video performance of Britten's *Young Person's Guide to the Orchestra*.

The teacher controlled the conditions under which pupils listened to the music, but did not insist on total silence. This left him free to suggest focuses for listening, ask pupils to make predictions, and give information about instruments, musical structure and modality at times when this was relevant to what the pupils could see and hear. He showed his delight in this piece of music, and his enthusiasm about sharing his knowledge.

The pupils responded with concentration and intellectual engagement. Some were clearly drawing constructively on previous learning about this piece of music at home or at primary school. Comments between pupils heard by the inspector included '... hope the violins are ready for their next bit ...' and 'isn't this the bit where the harp comes in?'

Like many other schools, Lawnswood School, Leeds, includes film music in its curriculum. At Lawnswood, pupils in Year 9 can absorb themselves in composing, performing and appraising film music for 80 minutes each week for half a term. The types of film music that they consider include music for silent film, incidental music and main title music. The range of contemporary films from which they watch relevant extracts includes *Part Time Pals* (Tom and Jerry), *The Wrong Trousers* (Wallace and Gromit) and *Superman II*. The musical features that they explore on keyboards, and try to include in at least one of their compositions, include pedal note, melodic fragment, repetition, sequence, chord cluster, ostinato, chromatic scale, and variation of dynamics, including silence.

As at many other schools, the curriculum at King Alfred's School, Wantage, includes a composition project based on advertising jingles. At King Alfred's, pupils undertake this project in their first term of Year 7. They have a clear understanding of the product they are advertising, and plan their use of the musical elements with the purpose of an advertisement clearly in mind. The teacher insists that all the sounds the pupils use are made with their voices. Their compositions are performed to the rest of the class with a sense of style and occasion, and show good understanding of the musical elements, good control of their voices, and the ability to make imaginative use of their voices.

In some schools there is an emphasis on the development of technical performance skills, and this is the core of the curriculum from which composing, listening and appraising activities grow.

At Gloucester School, a school in Germany for pupils with a parent working for the British armed forces, pupils learn to play touch-sensitive electronic keyboards very competently. Most pupils in Year 9 plan their fingering, and play pieces with four-note chords from staff notation fluently, expressively and accurately. There is similar attention to the development of keyboard

skills at The Ravensbourne School, Bromley. Pupils in Year 9 who are working on blues improvisations are expected to finger the chords, including added sixth chords, that they use.

Not all schools that emphasise the acquisition of technical skills focus on the use of electronic keyboards. At St John's RC School, Gravesend, pupils in Key Stage 3 use tuned and untuned percussion instruments of professional quality when performing and composing.

Some secondary schools emphasise the acquisition of vocal skills.

The Duchess's County High School, Northumberland, is a 13–18 school that emphasises singing. The pupils learn to sing unison songs, and in up to four parts. They are taught to sing in a range of styles and how to improve the quality of their singing. The popularity of singing in some Year 9 classes is illustrated by the examples of writing by pupils that are illustrated on page 76. The school promotes the image of singing as an adult musical activity. It is clear to the pupils that the music teacher enjoys singing. Pupils who are taking A-level music attend some Year 9 music lessons, and lead some of the singing.

Like Kates Hill Primary School, some secondary schools focus on the development of pupils' ability to internalise music. Visually impaired pupils at the RNIB New College, Worcester, perform compositions of substantial length from memory. When they refine their work, they remember the changes that they make reliably. They move neatly between the styles of playing required in the different sections of performances by anticipating changes and listening to each other closely and responsively.

Why I like Singing

When we sing in class, it is a way to use up our spare energy and everyone likes doing it. Singing is very pleasant, and when I do sing, I feel exceptionally spirited, endeavouring to do the best I can. There is a real atmosphere in the class when we sing, and it makes us try that much harder. I can't speak for everyone else, but I enjoy singing better than most other things in music. It gives me a chance to grasp what voice I have and pull it out of my mouth, trying the hardest I can most of the time.

A Year 9 boy at The Duchess's County High School explains why he enjoys singing

My View of singing

I quite like singing, not all songs though. I can't sing very high, but I can't sing very low either, sort of inbetween. I like singing 'Let it be' and 'Love is all around' more than 'Stome omeme o mali!' I don't know why exactly. Maybe because the people who wrote 'Love is all around' and 'Let it be' are people I've heard of, and that I already liked these songs before we sang them in school. I don't think I'd like singing in front of people that I don't know, but it would probably be worse in front of people that I do know. Singing on your own should be just like singing with a few other people, except if you had a few people singing with you, you would have someone to back you up, and make you feel more confident.

A Year 9 girl at The Duchess's County High School explains what she feels about singing

A Year 9 class at The Duchess's County High School rehearse a song

Year 7 pupils at Aylestone School rehearsing an arrangement of a song for performance to the class

The teaching described above is marked by high expectations of all pupils: in some cases pupils with differing abilities are set different tasks, and in others they work on the same task, but produce differing outcomes.

A few schools offer some extra music lessons for pupils who have been admitted to the school because of unusual ability or aptitude for music. Aylestone School, Hereford, is one such school. Since 1994, it has admitted a *music plus* group into Year 7. The Year 7 *music plus* pupils cover the National Curriculum in music by attending class music lessons alongside their peers. In addition, they receive some extra lessons, some of them out of school hours, that move beyond the requirements of the National Curriculum and are tailored to their needs and interests as well-motivated developing musicians. They are able to apply their musical skills, for example rehearsal skills, when they work with other pupils in class music lessons, and use these skills to help raise the attainment of all the pupils.

The hallmarks of music at Aylestone include the high expectations of teachers for all pupils, not just those who are members of the *music plus* group.

A lesson for seven pupils with learning difficulties in Year 7 focused on pentatonic scales. Working individually at keyboards, the pupils learnt to play a black-note pentatonic scale with their right hand, using sensible fingering, and added a given left hand part. They then improvised a left hand accompaniment, using chords, long notes and short notes. The lesson ended with the class learning to sing *Swing Low Sweet Chariot*. One of the pupils pointed out to the teacher that the melody is pentatonic.

Music in Key Stage 4 and post-16

ISSUES: participation in music at school; exploiting pupils' musical creativity and developing their musical imagination at post-16.

It is no coincidence that many of the secondary schools that were named in the previous section have a high level of participation in GCSE music. Schools where music is a popular choice at Key Stage 4 usually have good teaching and high standards in Key Stage 3.

William Parker School, Daventry, has increased the level of participation in music at Key Stage 4 substantially in recent years. In 1996 and 1997 over a quarter of pupils continued music. Pupils in Key Stage 3 know what to expect from GCSE music, because lessons in Key Stage 4 are not organised in a markedly different manner. The Key Stage 3 curriculum was planned to equip all pupils with the knowledge, understanding and skills that would allow any of them to continue music fruitfully in Key Stage 4.

A Year 8 class was working on a project on the differing characteristics of intervals. In the classroom, pupils were developing individual keyboard improvisations in ternary (ABA) form. The A section had to have a C/G drone and a melody in thirds, the B section a D/A drone and a melody in sixths. In the foyer, a group of percussionists worked on a ternary improvisation based on different drones, and with melodies in fifths and fourths. At the end of the lesson, interim performances of some pupils' work would be used to reinforce the differing effects of the *blended* intervals used by the keyboard players, and the *open* intervals used by the percussionists.

The keyboard players used patterns to shape their melodies, and made choices about tempo that they reconsidered when appropriate. They already knew how to record their drones into the keyboard memory, and play them back, so the teacher was able to concentrate on helping them to develop the musical qualities of their work. When she left the classroom to work with the percussionists the keyboard players remained engrossed in their task, just stopping occasionally to pass their headset to a friend, so that they could hear and comment on what they had done.

In addition to the quality of the teaching and the curriculum in Key Stage 3 there is another factor: the organisation of the choices between subjects that pupils make during Year 9. The school uses its option structure to communicate its vision of a balanced Key Stage 4 curriculum. In addition to the subjects that all pupils must take, they choose a humanities subject and an arts subject. They then choose a further subject, which can be a second modern foreign language, a second humanities subject, or a second arts subject. The message to parents and pupils is clear. At Key Stage 4 there are some subjects that all pupils must take. Beyond these, there are two areas of the curriculum, the humanities and the arts, which all pupils must continue, but where they can choose the subject in which they will specialise. Beyond that, pupils can decide whether to emphasise languages, humanities or the arts in their curriculum by making a free choice of a further subject.

Guthlaxton College, Leicester, is a 14–18 school, and so pupils choose their Key Stage 4 options with little direct experience of the music teaching that is available. Nevertheless, a recent change to the Key Stage 4 option system has encouraged more than 10 percent of the Year 10 pupils to choose GCSE music in 1997, and some additional pupils will take a one-year express course during Year 11.

At Tuxford School, Nottinghamshire, pupils in Year 9 are prepared to take the responsibility for their musical development that is necessary in Key Stage 4.

There was very little introduction to this Year 9 lesson: it was a free composition/performance project and the pupils knew what to do. Two groups of pupils listened to tracks on CDs they had brought from home, before starting to arrange a track of their choice. A group of seven pupils rehearsed a song around the piano, and three guitarists were arranging a pop song. Ten pupils worked in the recording studio on a song accompanied by electric guitar, bass guitar and drum kit. One pupil who wanted to work on her own at a keyboard did so.

The teacher tuned guitars for those having difficulty, and supervised the use of the recording studio. Nearly all the lesson was spent listening to the pupils' work, making informal assessments of their attainment and progress, and providing advice that was tailored to their needs. For example, the teacher showed the pupils who were singing round the piano how to give texture to their accompaniment by adding chords.

However popular GCSE music is at a school, many pupils cease to study music at the end of Year 9. Some schools provide a wide range of non-examination music courses that meet some of the musical needs of these pupils, and also stretch GCSE pupils.

At Wootton Upper School, Bedford, this provision includes lessons on the full range of orchestral instruments or voice, a wide range of ensembles, including two large percussion groups and a male voice choir, projects with visiting artists, and involvement in many national, regional and local events. Ensembles are often rehearsed by musicians who are employed specifically for this purpose. This removes some of the load on the school music teacher, and allows pupils to work with musicians with a wide range of expertise.

At Estover Community College, Plymouth, over 250 pupils regularly take part in lunchtime and after-school activities that range from wind bands to steel bands, African drumming and junk bands. Some of the ensembles have established a national and international reputation. Members of the local community participate in some of the ensembles.

The symphony orchestra of almost 80 pupils at Egglescliffe School, Stockton-on-Tees, plays an ambitious repertoire that challenges all the players. The orchestral players approach their work professionally. They arrive promptly for rehearsals before and after school, remember instructions that their conductor has given them only once, and play with expression and attention to balance and style even when they are sight-reading.

In some schools ensembles are initiated by

pupils with particular skills and interests, and then become part of the range of the activities that the school offers. The gospel singing at St Saviour's and St Olave's, Southwark, is an example of this. It began with a group of enthusiastic pupils who wanted a room to rehearse in at lunchtime. Over the years, teachers have been drawn in, public performances organised, and more pupils of all ages have started to participate. Pupils who take GCSE courses in music have sometimes offered gospel singing as part of their assessed work. The pupils who are expert gospel singers continue to take much of the responsibility for training singers, and developing their repertoire.

The final issue to be addressed in this section is closely related to one that was considered with reference to primary schools: exploiting pupils' musical creativity and developing their musical imagination. This is an issue for some pupils who are taking GCSE music courses in Key Stage 4, and for many of those who are on A-level courses at post-16. From their first days in Year 12, pupils' A-level courses may be fragmented into sub-courses that focus on specific A-level papers. Opportunities for pupils to develop their aural discrimination when they are performing, composing, or studying set works may be overlooked. Personal responses to music, based on pupils' musical experiences, may appear not to be valued at A-level.

Some schools have addressed this issue effectively.

Gospel singers at St Saviour's and St Olave's

The A-level music course at Hanley Castle High School, near Worcester, emphasises creative and imaginative work. From Year 7, some pupils show a sense of identity as composers in the interesting and original touches that they bring to their work. Pupils' compositions are often rehearsed by school ensembles, or performed at concerts. A-level pupils work on a one-to-one basis with a teacher who is a composer.

The stimulus of writing music that is intended for a public performance by known players, and is not motivated solely by an examination, often adds considerably to the musicality of the composition process. The extract shown on page 82 is part of a brass quintet that an A-level pupil at Alexandra High School, Sandwell, was composing for five known players including herself and her teacher.

A Year 9 Hanley Castle High School pupil composing

Year 9 Hanley Castle High School pupils composing

An extract from a composition by an A-level pupil at Alexandra High School

At Northampton School for Boys, the divisions that can mark lessons that are preparing pupils for different A-level papers are not present. Pupils may be called upon to apply and develop their aural and performance skills in any lesson.

> The lesson opened with the pupils singing a Bach chorale at sight securely, and without an accompaniment. This shared practical experience was used as a springboard for starting to analyse the chorale, agreeing some of its expressive qualities, and discussing the use of the elements of music to achieve these expressive qualities. The pupils then related what they had learnt to their own compositions.

Similar qualities mark the teaching at Skipton Girls' High School, North Yorkshire.

> One of the set works was Schubert's *Death and the Maiden* Quartet. After some work on the second movement, the two pupils and teacher rehearsed the *lied* that serves as its theme. One pupil played the piano, and the teacher and other pupil sang.
>
> The pupils had prepared themselves well for the lesson. They contributed effectively to the rehearsal, asserting their views about phrasing, asking and answering questions of each other, and working with the guidance of the teacher towards a commendable performance.

Good music teaching

This chapter has described some examples of good music teaching. The examples may be considered as pin-pricks of light into the good practice that may be found in many schools. The chapter has sought neither to name all the schools where there is good music teaching, nor to say all that could be said about the work in the schools that have been named. Neither is it intended to provide a template of good practice that all schools could adopt. No two schools are identical, and an idea that works in one school may not work elsewhere. However, the examples that have been given have some common qualities that could, arguably, be said to be the kernel of good music teaching. They include that:

- Music lessons include plenty of *musical activity*. We have included no examples of lessons where no music was heard, or where exercises that are silent, or require no more than reflex responses, were used to warm pupils up for musical activities that never transpired.

- Music lessons have a *clear teaching focus*, but are planned with an eye to the *full range of pupils' musical development*. The Year 2 lesson at Timothy Hackworth Primary School did not stop with the acquisition of knowledge about a song of Elton John, but also addressed the application of this knowledge to the pupils' compositions. The Year 12 lesson at Skipton Girls' High School did not stop with the making of verbal notes about a movement of a Schubert string quartet, but used practical work to develop pupils' understanding.

- Music lessons are *organised to promote learning*. All the music lessons cited attempted to *build on pupils' prior learning* and increase their musical knowledge, understanding and skills. We have included no examples of lessons that consisted of activities chosen only because they could be found on the next page of a scheme of work, or only because the pupils were thought likely to enjoy them.

- Music lessons are planned to cater for the *full spectrum of pupils' prior learning*. In the lessons cited, the teachers used strategies to ensure that all pupils had the opportunity to learn. In the Year 7 lesson at The Dormston School, explanations were given clearly, and pupils who were already familiar with Britten's *Young Person's Guide to the Orchestra* still had the opportunity to learn something new. In the nursery at Sheringham Primary School and during the Key Stage 2 lesson at Fountaindale Special School adults adapted their teaching to take account of the learning needs of individuals.

- Pupils are *taught the technical skills* that they need to develop and apply their knowledge of music. At Coseley School, Year 7 pupils were given advice about how to improve their singing. At Corbridge Middle School, pupils have workable techniques on several instruments. Year 6 pupils at Kates Hill Primary School tailor their compositions to match the techniques of the pupils who will perform their work.

- Pupils are taught to be more informed consumers of music. Whenever the pupils were played recorded music they were expected to *think about and analyse what they were hearing*. In line with the National Curriculum, and syllabuses for GCSE, the curriculum for pupils aged 5–16 years brought them into *informed and critical contact* with a *range of music* that could not typically be found on any single radio channel.

6 Concluding remarks

THIS book has painted an encouraging picture of arts education in schools in England. It has shown that there are many schools where one or more of the arts has reached a healthy stage of development, and where the teaching is good and set to improve further. There will be other schools with similar qualities that have not been included.

The essays on good teaching in art, dance, drama and music that form the core of this book have much in common. There are, however, notable differences that mark out the subject disciplines.

On one level, the common features of the four subject essays reflect the criteria that the *Framework for Inspection* (OFSTED 1995a) required the inspectors to use when they evaluated the teaching that they observed. These criteria are stated in Chapter 1 (page 2). Thus each chapter refers to some generic features of good teaching in all subjects, including effective planning and preparation, high expectations of pupils, and appropriate use of well-chosen resources.

At a deeper and more detailed level, the common features of the subject essays reveal some of the qualities of subject teaching in the arts that helps to improve the curriculum of schools, raises pupils' attainment, and enhances their progress. Good teaching in art, dance, drama and music:

- reflects the changing nature of arts subjects. None of these subjects is quite the same as it was ten years ago, or will be ten years hence. This is partly because society's expectations of schools change, and also because pupils change, teachers change and art forms change. A curriculum in art, dance, drama or music which is exactly the same as that offered ten years ago, or possibly only one year ago, does not reflect the dynamic nature of its subject;

- is informed by contemporary developments in artmaking and art forms. Those who work professionally in art, dance, drama or music may use ideas from the past, and almost certainly use skills from the past, but do not simply attempt to recreate the past, an aspiration which is in any case unattainable as the past means something different in the present. Professional artists test the boundaries of subject disciplines and art forms, the limits of their materials, the scope of new resources, for example information technology, and the openness and taste of their audiences. They use the language of their art forms to explore ethical issues, moral dilemmas, spirituality and their individuality. As they do this, their subjects change, sometimes expanding across subject boundaries or using new media, and at other times narrowing and becoming more focused. Progress as an artist is not necessarily equated with the use of an increasing range of media or art forms, or the crossing of subject boundaries. Fusion of the arts is natural in some cultures and contexts, and an aim of some artists working in other circumstances, perhaps at some particular points of their careers, but is clearly not a goal to which all artists must, should or do aspire;

- expects sustained enquiry and concentration. None of these subjects allows a passive response from pupils. Like professional artists, pupils must push forward the frontiers of their own work, reflect on and evaluate its outcomes, and learn from their successes and mistakes. The levels of accuracy and consistency that the arts require are exacting. There is no equivalent to correction fluid in many forms of artistic performance, or when working with some artistic media. An error rate of 1 percent in the performance of a well-known poem or passage or the notes of a familiar melody is often readily detectable;

- leads to the development of knowledge and understanding, and imparts the basic skills, the nuts and bolts, of the subject. The ability to observe primarily, but not only, using ears and eyes is crucial to artistic activity. Expression of one's ideas is impossible without adequate control of the media that one is using, for example a paintbrush, the voice or a musical instrument. The ways in which such skills are taught may change with the years, and can be adapted to suit the receptiveness of pupils and the preferences of teachers, but the need for the skills remains constant.

This book is OFSTED's first substantial published contribution to the development of the arts in schools. No matter how soon we write again, the arts will not be quite the same. Changes in professional arts practice, in the interpretation of the work of artists past and present, as well as the creation of new work, will lead to some adjustments, however subtle, in what is meant by good arts teaching. Many of the skills and much of the knowledge and understanding that needs to be taught will be the same as now, but the ways in which they are applied may change to reflect the dynamic nature of the arts.

List of schools visited

Abraham Guest High School, Wigan
Alderbrook High School, Solihull
Alexandra High School, Sandwell
Ash Green County Primary School, Staffordshire
Aylestone School, Hereford
Beauchamp Middle School, Bedfordshire
Bellevue Girls School, Bradford
Boughton Heath Primary School, Chester
Bridgewater County High School, Warrington
Brookside Primary School, nr Stockport
Broughton Junior School, North Lincolnshire
Castle High School, Dudley
Castleview Combined School, Slough
Chetham's School of Music, Manchester
Coates Endowed Middle School, Newcastle
Corbridge Middle School, Northumberland
Coseley School, nr Wolverhampton
Cross Hall High School, Ormskirk
Dartford Grammar School for Girls, Kent
Davison CE High School for Girls, West Sussex
Dorcan Comprehensive School, Swindon
Edmonton School, Enfield
Egglescliffe School, Stockton-on-Tees
Ellen Wilkinson High School, Manchester

Endon High School, Stoke-on-Trent
Enfield Grammar School, Middlesex
Estover Community College, Plymouth
Fountaindale Special School, Mansfield
Gloucester School, Germany
Guthlaxton College, Leicester
Hanley Castle High School, nr Worcester
Harthill County Primary, Chester
Hextable School, Kent
High Storrs Secondary School, Sheffield
Highfields School, Wolverhampton
Intake High School, Leeds
Kates Hill Primary School, Dudley
King Alfred's School, Wantage
King Offa Junior School, Bexhill-on-Sea
Lawnswood School, Leeds
Linton Village College, Cambridgeshire
Longfield Middle School, Harrow
Longmead Primary School, Hillingdon
Lucas Vale Primary School, Lewisham
Martin Wilson Primary School, Shrewsbury
Meadow Vale Primary School, Bracknell
Minster School, Southwell
Neston County High School, South Wirral
Newbiggin-by-the-Sea Middle School, Northumberland
Newfield School, Sheffield

Northampton School for Boys
Our Lady and Pope John XXIII School, Corby
Our Lady of the Wayside RC School, Solihull
Overleigh St Mary's Primary School, nr Chester
Park Community School, Hampshire
Park House School, Berkshire
Pashley Down Infant School, Eastbourne
Penketh High School, Warrington
Pipworth Junior School, Sheffield
Poynton High School, Cheshire
Purcell School, Harrow
Rainsford High School, Essex
Ringmer Community College, West Sussex
RNIB New College, Worcester
Roedean School, Brighton
Roxbourne Middle School, Harrow
Sharnbrook Upper School and Community College, Bedfordshire
Sherard Primary School, nr Melton Mowbray
Sheringham Primary School, Norfolk
Skipton Girls' High School, North Yorkshire
Springwell School, Staveley
St Gregory's RC High School, Warrington
St John's RC School, Gravesend
St Michaels CE High School, Sandwell
St. Peter's CE Primary School, Harrogate

St Saviour's and St Olave's School, Southwark
Stamford Park Junior School, Trafford
The Bishops' CE High School, Chester
The BRIT Performing Arts and Technology School, Croydon
The Dormston School, Dudley
The Duchess's County High School, Alnwick
The Hill Primary School, Thurnscoe, Barnsley
The Ravensbourne School, Bromley
Theale Green School, Reading
Thorns School and Community College, Dudley
Timothy Hackworth Primary School, Shildon
Trinity CE High School, Manchester
Tudhoe Grange Comprehensive School, Co Durham
Tuxford School, Nottinghamshire
Wells Cathedral School, Somerset
West Derby School, Liverpool
William Parker School, Daventry
William Tyndale Primary School, Islington
Wingfield Comprehensive School, Rotherham
Wootton Upper School, Bedford
Worden High School, Preston
Worsbrough High School (now renamed Elmhirst School), Barnsley
Yehudi Menuhin School, Cobham

List of references

Arts Council of England (1997), *Arts Organisations and their Education Programmes*.

Department for Education (1995), *The National Curriculum*, HMSO.

Department for Education & Employment and Office for Standards in Education (1997), *The Quality of Education in Nursery Voucher Settings*.

Department of National Heritage (1996), *Setting the Scene: The Arts and Young People*.

Gardiner, M.F., Fox, A., Knowles, F. and Jeffrey, D. (1996), 'Learning Improved by Arts Training', *Nature*, 381, p284.

Hertrich, J. A. (1997), *Standards in English 1995–96*, distributed by NATE, NAAE.

Jones, P. (1997), *Art: A Review of Inspection Findings 1995–96*, AAIDE/Dudley LEA publications.

Mills, J. (1997a), 'Office for Standards in Education Music Inspection Findings (Primary)', *Primary Music Today*, 8, pp 20–21.

Mills, J. (1997b), 'Music Inspections 1995–96 – Main Findings (Secondary)', YES, 26, pp3–5.

Munsch R.N. (1982), *The Paper Bag Princess*, Scholastic.

National Council for Educational Technology (NCET) (in press), *Fusion: Art and IT in Practice*, NCET.

Office for Standards in Education (1993), *Music: Key Stages 1, 2 and 3: First Year 1992–93*, HMSO.

Office for Standards in Education (1995a), *Framework for the Inspection of Schools*, HMSO.

Office for Standards in Education (1995b), *Music: A Review of Inspection Findings 1993–94*, HMSO.

Office for Standards in Education (1996a), *Subjects and Standards: Key Stages 1 and 2*, HMSO.

Office for Standards in Education (1996b), *Subjects and Standards: Key Stages 3 and 4 and Post-16*, HMSO.

School Curriculum and Assessment Authority (1996a), *Desirable Outcomes for Children's Learning on Entering Compulsory Education*.